Yeshua Buddha

Cover art by *Jane A Evans*

Yeshua Buddha

*An interpretation of New Testament
theology as a meaningful myth.*

JAY G. WILLIAMS

This publication made possible
with the assistance of the Kern Foundation

The Theosophical Publishing House
Wheaton, Ill. U. S. A.
Madras, India/London, England

Library of Congress Cataloging in Publication Data
Williams, Jay G.   1932
    Yeshua Buddha: an essay in Christian mythology.

    (Quest books)
    Includes bibliographical references and index.
    1. Jesus Christ—Theosophical interpretations.
    2. Myth. I. Title.
          BT304.97.W54   232   78-8789
                  ISBN 0-8356-0515-9

TO HERMINE

Wir Menschen alle, wir Anspruchsvolleren, wir mit
der Gehnsucht, mit der Dimension zuviel, könnten
gar nicht leben, wenn es nicht ausser der Luft dieser
Welt auch noch eine andre Luft zu atmen gäbe, wenn
nicht ausser der Zeit auch noch die Ewigkeit bestünde,
und die ist das Reich des Echten.

(All we who ask too much and have a dimension too
many could not contrive to live at all if there were not
another air to breathe outside the air of this world, if
there were not eternity at the back of time; and this is
the kingdom of truth.)

Hermann Hesse, *Steppenwolf*

CONTENTS

CONTENTS

PREFACE

The purpose of this book is to present in brief compass what may seem to many a radically different understanding of the man who has been known in the Western world as Jesus Christ but who is named here, for the purpose of this discussion, "Yeshua Buddha." Perhaps a word should be said first about this title.

Despite the universal use of the name "Jesus" in English-speaking countries, Yeshua is undoubtedly closer to his original name as it would have been pronounced in first century Palestine. I have used Yeshua here, however, not out of antiquarian interest but because the name Jesus bears so much emotional freight that it cannot be uttered without provoking a variety of immediate visceral reaction. I, myself, find it salutory to use the name Yeshua, if only because it allows me to think more clearly about the reality which stands behind the name.

The title, "Buddha," means "the Enlightened One" and, with that in mind, is appropriately applied to Yeshua who, throughout the New Testament, is described as the light of the world. It is also used in this volume to indicate that behind the interpretation of Yeshua here presented lies an approach which is similar in some respects to Eastern philosophy, particularly Buddhism. For the sake of simplicity, few technical Buddhist terms have been employed in the text itself, but those acquainted with that philosophical tradition will immediately recognize the use of such concepts of *anatta* (no self), *ancitta* (impermanence), and *nirvana* (no thingness). Furthermore, the truth of the following propositions is presupposed: (1) Life is *dukkha*, i.e., ephemerally disquieting, (2) The cause of life's disquietude is craving (*tanha*) or what the Greeks might have called *eros*. (3) Man craves because he is entrapped by the illusion of the ego, and (4) The cord of craving can be broken only by the dispelling of that ego illusion. For those who wish to pursue these and other Buddhist ideas further and in more depth notes have occasionally been provided. Since parallels between Christianity and certain forms of Mahayana Buddhism seem most obvious, the text has been keyed primarily to the Mahayana tradition.

Lest there be any misunderstanding, however, let it be said at the outset that the point is not to demonstrate that Yeshua was influenced by Buddhist thought or even that he and Gautama Siddhartha taught the same thing. Rather, the intention is to explore the possibility that Yeshua represents a way to enlightenment which is neither Western nor Eastern but universal and perennial, a way which is usually misunderstood by Christian theologians.

I am keenly aware, of course, that in this exploration a methodology and hermeneutic is employed which will hardly appeal to large segments of the scholarly community. Little attention is paid to the historical background of the New Testament or to modern critical analysis. Quotations from the Synoptic Gospels and John are mixed together without much distinction. No interest is shown in distinguishing among the different theologies of the four Gospel writers or the various "sources" with which they worked. Form criticism is not even mentioned.

This is because, as shall be explained more fully in Chapter I, the Gospel is taken in this study as a "mythological whole." The intent is not historical reconstruction or even discovery of the "original meaning" of the text. The Gospels are for the present and are read accordingly. Hence, this is no objective, scholarly examination of ancient documents for the sake of pure knowledge. The undergirding question continually is: What does the Gospel mean now? How can we read these ancient documents coherently, so that they will make sense?

My thesis is that the "perennial philosophy,"[1] so well represented in Asia by Buddhism, provides a significant perspective from which to understand the life and teachings of Yeshua. Many readers, of course, will undoubtedly question a methodology which imposes foreign categories upon a text. My response to such an objection is two-fold. First, it seems clear that no interpreter can help but impose categories foreign to Scripture upon the Bible. If one looks at the history of exegesis one finds Jewish, Platonic, Neo-Platonic, Aristotelian, humanistic, occult, existentialist and pragmatic interpretations, to mention only a few. Even those modern interpreters who wish to dispense entirely with all imposed metaphysical or interpretive presuppositions operate with a hidden agenda. It is not surprising that anti-metaphysical ways of reading the Bible arose precisely at the time when philosophy itself had turned against metaphysics. It is true that some worldviews cohere more reasonably with the New Testament than others, but the idea that a modern man can think like a first century man is suspect if only because first century men did not normally try to think like their predecessors.

Second, those foreign categories which have been selected for use have been chosen not just because they are a part of our modern *Weltanschaung* (which they are not) but because they appear to be true. If they are such, they ought to cohere with whatever truth there may be in Christian Scriptures. The essential argument of this book is that such coherence does exist and that Yeshua is, in truth, Buddha.

I should say at the outset, however, that my aim is not to answer all scholarly questions or to deal with all possible objections to this position. To do so would be to produce a work of enormous length and detail which could be appreciated only by other scholars rather than one which can be read in one sitting by fishermen and tax collectors.

Not that all conceptions in the book are easily grasped. Some fisherman may find Chapter 1 difficult going, though anyone who has felt the swirling waters of the sea under him will have some appreciation of what is going on. On the whole, I have tried to write simply and briefly, with the hope that the kernel of the argument will be apparent to all who wish to understand.

At the same time, I believe the position outlined can be defended against major objections and am quite willing to enter into dialogue about it in the future. My hope is that this little work will at least stimulate discussion about the real, earth-shattering meaning of the Gospel. If that happens, I shall be more than satisfied.

One word more should be said to the women who read this book. English is a clumsy language to use, for inevitably one is put into the position of referring to a person of either sex as "he." I trust that you will understand that the fault lies more with the language and less with me. Whenever you read the masculine pronoun you may substitute the feminine form if you like. Certainly you should understand that words like "Adam" and "Man" refer to both men and women without distinction.

Jay G. Williams
Hamilton College, N.Y.

1

THEOS: A PROLEGOMENA

T he term *theology*, when taken at face value, appears as at best paradoxical and at worst nonsensical. It means, basically, talking about, thinking about, reasoning about,*Theos* .[1] *Theos*, however, is precisely that which can be neither described nor objectified. All *logoi*[2] are designed to elucidate aspects of the cosmos, to put in order some realm of sense experience which men share in common. *Theos*, on the other hand, is known neither through external nor internal experience. *Theos* is not an object, not even the most lofty and spiritual object. If one uses the word "exist" as it is employed in ordinary language, it ought never to be applied to *Theos*, for *Theos*, unlike tables, persons, countries, and elementary particles, does not "stand forth" (exist) for man.

Hence, theology, though it rhymes with geology, biology, and sociology, is hardly a science of the same order and ought not to be confused with them. Human sciences deal with facts, i.e., with what has been done (*facio*, to make or do). Thus all sciences explore the past, the structured world of *facta*. In this sense, all sciences are essentially historical.[3] *Theos*, on the other hand, exists in neither past nor future, for *Theos* is never *factum* (made or done) nor will *Theos* ever become so. Theology which patterns itself after other human sciences, therefore, is bound to be confused if not foolish. The attempt to metamorphose *Theos* into an objective thing can only have the effect of presenting God as dead, for all "things" are dead.

Trying to understand *Theos* as a "principle" or "concept" is

13

even more absurd for there is nothing abstract about *Theos* at all. *Theos* cannot even be conceived by human intellect. One of the great tragedies of Western theology is that it became entangled at an early date with metaphysics, a perfectly justifiable science in its own right, which abstracts certain general concepts from the other sciences.[4] Terms like being and becoming, form and matter, substance and accidents, may not be very useful for modern physics but they represent an ancient, though now dated attempt to express certain basic principles which lie behind the physics. Today such notions find their counterparts in concepts such as natural law, matter and anti-matter, probability, relativity, etc.

In any event, if *Theos* is not a part of the dead world of *facta*, *Theos* surely is not a part of that set of abstract ideas which men have derived from (or impressed upon) the world of facts. Any attempt, therefore, to understand *Theos* as some principle of motion or to equate *Theos* and Being (or the Ground of Being) is doomed to have disastrous consequences.[5] *Theos* is neither formal, material, efficient, nor final cause. *Theos* is neither he-ness, she-ness, it-ness, nor even is-ness.

If such is the case, one must ask how theology can exist at all. Or was A. J. Ayer correct when he consigned religion and religious language to the realm of emotional outburst?[6] Before we can begin to answer this question it may be well to explore some of the bald and perhaps troubling assertions already made, to see what they really imply. In so doing, let us consider first that realm of facts which, when taken as a whole, constitutes the cosmos and which, when regarded experientially, appears to us in space and time.

Perhaps the first observation which must be made is one already alluded to, i.e., that everything we experience is already past and dead. The truth of this statement is made clear by thinking about the stars which appear to us at night. Although in one sense we see the stars, what we actually perceive is light which in some instances, was emitted from objects several millennia ago. Many of these celestial objects which we "see" no longer "exist" in any perceivable form for they have long since exploded. Looking into the sky, is looking into the far distant past; astronomy is a form of history.

When we turn our eyes to closer celestial objects like the sun and moon or to terrestrial phenomena the time lag is shortened considerably—but it is always there. That which we see or hear or smell or touch has already changed by the time we sense it. We never see what is, only what was. Moreover, the closer one gets to objects, the more fleeting and impermanent they appear. The table before me, for instance, seems relatively solid and unchangeable. An examination of the atomic and subatomic structure of the table, however, reveals a constantly changing, even unpredictable set of phenomena.

What one discovers is that those forms of reality which we perceive with our ordinary senses are arbitrary constructions which appear only when the world is looked at from a particular point of view. When examined by the physicist even the most solid objects appear to be largely empty space. Flat surfaces turn out to be anything but flat. Permanence is but a visual illusion masking constant flux.[7]

At the same time, we must also admit that our vision of the atomic and subatomic worlds is no less imaginary than the ordinary world of desks and chairs. Indeed, that whole elaborate world of atomic physics so artfully depicted in science textbooks is but a construct designed to put in order certain phenomena. In order to see it, one must exercise the imagination rather vigorously, for it is a way of visualizing the invisible. The physicist is consigned to work with the trail which has been left behind; only his imagination can reconstruct how the beast which made such tracks might have looked.

Second, not only is all experience—both external and internal—of the past. It is also thoroughly shaped and conditioned by our special, human sensory apparatus, our cultural background, and our own individual experience. We can hardly imagine how the world would appear if we had different senses, say eyes sensitive to "cosmic rays" or noses which could pick up the emission of radioactive particles. Yet such *could* be the case. What we see and know is as much shaped by our own sensory and conceptual apparatus as it is by the so-called external world.[8] In effect, what we perceive are certain relatively consistent reactions to the inexplicable which our senses provide for us. It must be recognized that these received messages are no more "like" their causes than a letter is "like" its sender. Because it is simply impossible to know the "cause" apart from sensory experience, however, we are consigned to speak about only the sensorially created world which we know through experience. The cosmos, then, is like a very complicated and many-sided series of messages sent from the unknown which we are compelled to translate in our own terms. These messages are to man reality (thing-ness); their source, nonreality (no thing-ness).[9]

Man's translation of these messages never takes place in a vacuum but is thoroughly conditioned by his situation within a particular human culture. Indeed, the cosmos appears to the infant as a confusing series of inexplicable stimuli until language teaches him to put the world in some sort of order. The vast multiplicity of human languages attests to the added fact that every linguistic ordering is, at least in part, arbitrary.

The relation between language and fact is, at root, circular. It is true that language is shaped by the cosmos around us, but it is equally true that language also shapes decisively the cosmos perceived. For instance, we receive perceptual messages which we describe as pink. We see pink. At the same time, many ancient languages had no word for such a color, a sign that among those people pink was not visually distinguished from, say, red and hence was not seen as such. The question then is: To what extent do we "see" pink because we have a word for it? Recourse to spectral analysis does not really solve the problem for we do not see light waves of a particular length. We see colors.

The extent to which language affects our actual perception of the cosmos becomes painfully evident when one attempts to learn a new language as different from English as some form of Bantu or Chinese. Although translations can be made, one soon discovers that they can never be more than rough approximations, for there is no one-to-one correspondence between languages in the realm of either vocabulary or syntax. To say, for instance, that *ming* means fate or *jen* means human-heartedness is comparable in exactness to saying Peking Duck means Roast Long Island Duck. There is *some* truth in what is said, but the inexactness must not be glossed over. Just as American cooking has nothing quite like Peking Duck, so American vocabulary has nothing which means the same as *ming* and *jen*. Moreover, in language, as in cooking, it is the subtlety of taste rather than some generalized correspondence which really matters.

Language, of course, is but one aspect of the way in which culture shapes perception and our vision of reality. Indeed, most of those elements of life which men regard as particularly important are, no more than commonly agreed upon fantasies. For instance, a nation, though generally regarded as an important aspect of reality, has no substance apart from what the imagination of men gives it. The border between the United States and Canada is "there" only in so far as men have commonly agreed to imagine that it is there. A boundary is like a goal line in football. It serves its purpose as a result of common agreement about the rules of the game. When people stop playing the game, it disappears instantly as a functioning part of reality.

To be sure, such fantasies about nations have all sorts of important and very real consequences, but they are still fantasies. Nations will only exist as long as men imagine that they do. They are always "of" if not always "by and for" the people. To think that the United States of America has some sort of objective reality which exists apart from men is folly.

The same may be said of that other powerful ingredient in modern, secular society: money. Money, essentially, has no value in and of itself; it is worth something only by common consent. That is to say, the value of a dollar is only what people pretend it is. Alexander Hamilton's picture intrinsically has no more value than George Washington's.

To be sure, there are many factors which influence this game of "Let's Pretend." Men can't change the rules of the game by whim, for the power of consensus is very strong. Still, so-called real money is more like the bills in a game of Monopoly than most people would care to admit. That is, it finds its reality exclusively within the realm of human imagination.[10]

One could extend this list of examples indefinitely—even into the sacred realms of mathematics and natural science—but in this brief, opening synopsis there is no need to indulge ourselves in elaboration. It is enough to say, by way of asserting the basic position to be taken in this volume, that man lives his life in an imaginary world of human construction. Although he shares this realm of fantasy with other human beings (and it is this agreement which gives his imaginings solidity and power) there is seldom absolutely universal agreement about such imagined rules and realities. Hence, human life is characterized by the intermittent struggle between men and societies who do not commonly agree about the imagined realms.

Finally, we must say a word—but no more than a word—about the differences in perception which exist among individuals. Obviously, different persons from the same culture can look at what would seem to be the very same data and see quite different things. As the old adage goes, "One man's meat is another man's poison." This is literally true both in a biological and in a psychological sense. Sensory data do not affect men uniformly. Each of us brings his own "slant" which sharply or mildly distinguishes him from his neighbors. Each individual imagination shapes reality and presents it uniquely. In fact, it is misleading even to speak about the *same* sensory data. Apart from the individual no data can be known. "Same" means only that an impressive number of individuals receive sensations which they describe in very similar ways.[11]

When an individual's imagination differs too decisively from that of his peers he may be branded eccentric, deluded, or even insane. Such labels have, to be sure, limited and pragmatic justification. The insane person is, in a way, like someone who insists upon playing Hearts when the other three players at his table are engaged in a game of Bridge. Obviously, neither he nor his imagination fits the situation and can only be described as disruptive. On the other hand, it must always be remembered that in another situation his imagination might be quite in place and that the other three would then be disruptive.

In our society a person who constantly insisted that he could fly into the heavens to see the gods and spirits would probably eventually be placed in a mental institution. Certainly, he would never be licensed as a physician. Among shamanistic people, on the contrary, he might well be accorded a place of honor and sought out for his curing powers.[12] Conversely, these same shamanistic peoples might well show contempt for the Western physician who knows nothing of the realm of the spirit.

Basically, then, the point is this: the cosmos which we see and know and live in is provisionally "there" but ultimately an illusion. It is the now past and dead result of the interaction between the unknown and our own, somewhat arbitrary imagination. The cosmos may be described as consentual reality—reality which is commonly agreed to for the purpose of playing the game of life. It is always possible, however, to imagine a different covenant of consent and hence a different world.

The notion that the world we share is ultimately illusory is, admittedly, strong medicine which needs further amplification if it is to be swallowed at all. By illusion is not meant something entirely worthless or unimportant. Needless to say, nations, wealth, and mathematics are all significant features of modern human life. Rather, illusion ought to be understood as like the illusions of a game or play. We share together the illusion of the cosmos and in so doing are able to relate to each other. Life, the game in which we are involved, is serious and vastly important though perhaps not in the way most believe. Without life's fantasies we could not communicate with each other at all. Life would simply fall apart. It would be like a school recess without any games or customs or civilities to provide order. Nevertheless, to become so wrapped up in the game that one fails to see its arbitrary nature is a fatal mistake. The cosmos is finally finite, ephemeral, arbitrary, past, and dead.

Once the cosmos has been discovered for what it is, i.e., revelation from the unknown so profoundly shaped by human imagination that it bears no resemblance to its "source," the tendency and temptation are to retreat into the ego as the source for ultimate reality.[13] Here, too, however, we are bound to encounter insurmountable obstacles, for the ego, like the rest of the cosmos, is known only as past, only as imagined reality, and hence only as illusion.

The ego is a part of the cosmos. Internal feelings and thoughts are as much perceptions as external sensations. The ultimate dichotomy is not between the ego and the cosmos nor between the internal and the external. The ego is an aspect of the cosmos and obeys its laws. The internal is on a continuum with the external. The only dichotomy which is of significance is that dichotomy between something and no thing.

What do I know about my ego? What is this "self" with which

19

I seem to be bound? Basically, what I know of myself is what I have perceived myself to have been. That is, my ego-concept is of what is already dead and gone, of where I was but no longer am. It is as though I were riding on the back of an observation car of a train and, seeing the tracks where I have ridden, identified myself with them. One of life's primary illusions is to succumb to the temptation to cling to this self-constructed illusion, the ego, as reality.[14]

The tracks stretch out to the horizon behind me and I gaze at them, believing that I am contemplating my very self. As I do so, however, my view is thoroughly shaped by what society tells me I ought to see. The ego is at least partially formed by my society's view of sex, family, beauty, vocation, etc. Clearly, my ego itself is a product of our corporate and my individual imagination. Hence, it is perilous to search for the ultimate, i.e., the non-illusory, within the confines of the ego. The ego is a part of the cosmos, that many-splendored dance which takes place before our eyes. The ego, like all those other objects which surround us, is an aspect of the world of ten thousand things and can only be understood as such.

With what then are we left? A created, imagined world in which the ego itself takes its part; history, the past, the dead; the world of science. Is that not enough? Can anything more be known than that? Should we not be content to know only what is available for knowledge? In one sense, yes, it is enough. At least, it is all the world that we can know, for knowledge presupposes the past. This is the only world with which our minds can deal intelligibly.

Furthermore, from the point of view of science it is best not to look further. The natural and social sciences have rightly discarded such notions as "God" and the "Soul" as extraneous and disruptive.[15] Science can get on quite well without the importation of the notion of the Absolute as some sort of *deus ex machina*.

Hence theology ought to leave those realms of human knowledge called the arts and sciences essentially alone. Like the game of chess, physics needs no particular improvement upon its rules nor even any lofty justification for its existence. If theology has anything at all to say to human science it is only a reminder of the arbitrary and "ludenic"[16] nature of all such enterprises. Even at that a theologian must use restraint; it is rather annoying to a chess master to be told repeatedly and with a slight indication of contempt that in China and Japan chess has different rules. Nevertheless, beside such reminders theology offers no positive contribution to the advancement of human knowledge at all.

Theology points to the unspeakable, the unimaginable, the unknown and hence can never be classed as a form of human knowledge. Still, it is precisely the unknown which the cosmos presupposes at every moment. We live in a world created by our senses and our intellect, yet not wholly created. What is this unknown which sends us messages of blue, heavy, and damp?

Until fairly recently Western philosophy named this unknown, "substance," and then proceeded to make all sorts of pronouncements about it. Contemporary philosophy, as an objective science, has quite rightly attacked the concept of substance as meaningless and has generally refused to speculate in such a manner. Substance, like that proverbial tortoise upon which, according to the ancients, the world-supporting elephant stands, is a nugatory principle of explanation, for it explains nothing. Nevertheless, the idea that the world we sense is like the pre-sensed world is equally foolish. Talk about this unknown may be absurd and should certainly never intrude into a scientific discussion; yet it seems inevitable nonetheless.[17]

All knowledge is of the past and dead; we can know only facts and theories about those facts. Without the present, however, the past makes no sense at all. Without the present there can be no before or after, no done or to be done, no here or there. Without the present, the here and now, the whole panorama of history collapses into nothing. By the present, I do not mean that infinitely thin dividing line between what has been and what will be.[18] The present is not on a continuum with past and future but stands over against them as their creator.

The future, of course, is nothing more than a way of imagining what the past will be like after it has occurred. It is as formed as the past. The present, on the other hand, is unconceived, unformed, and always the same. "Now" does not change but endures; it is the fixed point by which all other temporal points are defined. Even in saying that, however, the truth is distorted. The moment one begins to speak univocally about that which all knowledge presupposes, an object is created and that of which we speak is lost in the world.

The present can never become an object because all objects are past, for the present to be past is a contradiction in terms. This does not mean, however, that that of which we speak is foolishness. On the contrary, then presupposes now; there presupposes here; the cosmos presupposes the unknown. "Suchness," if I may use the Buddhist term, is that which makes all things possible.[19] It becomes nonsensical, however, the moment it becomes "it." To speak, to theologize, then, is to disrupt and mislead.

Is there then no way to speak theologically? Are we left only with the silence prescribed by Lao Tzu in the *Tao Teh Ching*?[20] Must the theologian as theologian respond to all questions with muteness? with an unknowing smile? with the dull glance of an idiot? Would it not be simpler to abstain from theology entirely and plunge unthinkingly into the cosmic dance?

Two avenues remain open to the theologian, though neither is unequivocal. The first has been called in the Western world the *via negativa* and in the East *neti neti*.[21] That is, the theologian can do in essence what we have done thus far in this chapter, maintaining repeatedly that *theos* is neither this nor that and by so doing defending *theos* from misinterpretation. Thus, *theos* is neither spatial nor non-spatial, neither temporal nor non-temporal, neither personal nor impersonal, neither finite nor infinite. Ultimately this approach results in the assertion that *theos* has no properties, cannot be described, is neither real nor unreal, does not exist. Or, to put it another way, this avenue suggests that language cannot describe *theos* at all.

The second approach to *theos* is through myth. Let us define myth simply as a story or set of stories which point beyond themselves to *theos*. Nothing in a myth should be taken as unequivocally describing *theos*; yet everything in it may be seen as intimating, suggesting, pointing toward *theos*.[22]

This point must be kept in the forefront of our minds because many myths introduce the gods or God as characters in the story. These deities may be described in vivid detail; many actions and attitudes may be ascribed to them. In studying and rehearsing myths, however, we must always remember to understand such supernatural characters as pointers to the unknown. They are not themselves to be equated with the unknown. The truth of a myth lies in the interaction of the characters and what it intimates rather than in the literal description of the gods.

True myths are written for no apparent reason; they are neither propaganda nor theology. They are not designed to present facts or theories. Rather, they are natural expressions of man's relation to the unknown. They grew out of the depths of human experience in much the same way as a hair grows out of the head.[23] Myths have neither authors nor absolutely fixed forms but can be traced back through the generations until their roots are lost in the mists of antiquity. Over the centuries, a myth will be re-clothed repeatedly in the garments of each age; yet essentially will remain the same.

Myths are not to be treated as conveyors of beliefs or opinions and hence should not be destroyed through dissection and analysis in search for the same. Myths should be told and retold, for it is in the retelling, in the speaking and the hearing, that their meaning lies. At the same time, the theologian often feels compelled to extrapolate and expand upon his own received tradition as he witnesses to the meaning and the truth which he finds intimated within it. If he has any task at all it is to witness to the compelling power and splendor of myth.

Myths, of course, exist in the cosmos, as a part of human culture, and thus can also be dealt with scientifically. Some may find it interesting to understand a myth in terms of its particular historical setting, psychological motivation or sociological situation. For instance, the Gospel of Mark may be read as a product of a struggling Jewish sect which emerged in the first century A.D. One can compare the historical facts contained in the Gospels with what we know about the period from other sources. One can analyze the language, describe the cosmology, separate fact and fiction. Given our society's interest in historical factuality and scientific explanation all this seems quite predictable. It must be underlined, however, that such studies have little or nothing to do with the work of the theologian. It is regrettable, therefore, that so many Biblical "theologians" devote themselves almost exclusively to such tasks.

A myth is a living reality, not a dead museum piece. Hence, the search for its "original meaning"—if there ever was one—is quite beside the point. Mythologically speaking, it makes no difference whether the events described in the story actually took place or not. What matters is the myth as a finger pointing to the unknown. The discovery of a sworn statement signed by five hundred first century Jewish Rabbis attesting to the veracity of the resurrection stories found in the Gospels would have no effect at all upon the truth of the myth of the resurrection of Yeshua. Truth and factuality are entirely different—no matter what many modern philosophers may say.[24]

Such a view of the relation between myth and history is, of course, predicated upon the provisional assumption that history in some sense deals with reality "as it was." So engrained is this notion in our common sense that perhaps we must "let it be." There are reasons to suspect, however, that even the most "objective" sort of history is far more of a projection of the values and ideas of the historian than we usually recognize. The best way to see such a projection is to read virtually any old history text book. Almost immediately—and I care not what such book you pick up—the prejudices of the historian leap from the page in the most disconcerting way. Time has dissolved the common sense which once was shared by historian and reader and the work appears as what it is: an attempt to communicate or buttress a particular worldview by using the medium of abstractions which we term facts.

The distinction between myth and history, then, is not at all the distinction between fiction and fact. Rather, it is a distinction between a story (either fictional or factual) which points to the ineffable mysteries and a story which demonstrates in its telling abstract principles or an ideology.

The theologian as theologian does not worry about the factuality or fictional nature of a particular myth. Neither does he attempt to weed out "later additions" to the text as though those who added to the story were worthless corrupters of the tradition. Rather the myth is accepted as it stands. The theologian is but a finger pointing to a finger pointing.

Needless to say, accepting the myth "as it stands" is a somewhat tricky business. Translations are always just that and may, in fact, present a different myth from that known centuries ago. Actually, there never is just one myth, for myths are constantly transformed as age follows age. There simply is no way to get back to the original myth for that quest itself is a sign of a particular age. The theologian can only take the myth as he receives it and read it with his own eyes, for his own time.

Above all, he must beware lest he becomes trapped in the net of historicism. Nothing could be more damaging to theology than the reduction of myth to a series of pious sentiments or brilliant insights offered long ago at a particular time, for a particular people. If a myth does not mean now, it does not mean anything. It is not a myth.

Such, briefly, is the way in which theology and its work will be understood in this volume. The remaining chapters will be devoted to an exposition of specifically Christian mythology through a rereading of essential portions of the Gospel myth. For these purposes, the following texts have been chosen for special scrutiny:

> The Prologue to the Gospel of John (John 1:1-14)
> The Story of Yeshua's Baptism and Testing (Matt. 3:1-17)
> The Sermon on the Mount (Matt. 5:1 - 7:29)
> The Sending of the Twelve (Matt. 10:1-15)
> The Recognition of Yeshua as Christ at Caesarea Philippi and the Transfiguration (Matt. 16:13 - 17:8)
> The Passion Story (Mark 11:1 - 15:41)
> The Resurrection (Mark 15:42 - 16:8)

Other passages of Scripture might well have been added to this list, but it would seem that the essential gospel story can be found here, in these seven "moments."

The intent, of course, is not to provide a full exegesis of each text. That would detract from the essential purpose, for the aim is simply to see whether the Gospel can be understood adequately from the central point of view already partially summarized in the introduction and in this chapter. Nevertheless, we must work carefully, for the theological position under consideration is a radical, if perennial one. Certainly it goes against the grain of much modern theologizing and seems to stand much more in the tradition of Eastern mysticism rather than Western thought. To find such a position useful for the clarification of the Gospel story may either astound or annoy many.

It should be stressed that the object is not to prove that the Gospel writers of Yeshua were also believers in this perennial philosophy. In a sense, once a myth is formed, the original intent of the author becomes superfluous. One should not think of meaning as something ever to be found in the text itself. On the contrary, a myth's meaning emerges anew in each age and for each individual. Meaning is born out of the interaction among the story, the ego, and the unknown present. Hence there is no one meaning to any myth. That is the reason why myths have the capacity to endure through the ages. A myth with one fixed interpretation is bound to decay and soon be forgotten.

This essay in Christian mythology, then, should be taken as a product of an age in which West has met East and imperialism has been shown for what it is. This is not meant to be an imperialistic book in which Christianity conquers the heathen. It is rather an essay which hopefully will lay the foundation for fruitful mutual understanding between East and West. In it Yeshua and Gautama join hands to shed a common light into a darkened cosmos.

2

LOGOS

M yths come in a variety of forms, shapes, and sizes, yet most feature a hero who progresses perilously but relentlessly toward his goal.[1] This hero acts out the part of the ego we all know so well; yet he acts transparently so that the forces of destiny which empower him, test him, and impell him on his way are intimated if not revealed. The hero appears as the ego who dispels in his triumph the ego-illusion which traps mankind.

Some myths provide a supernatural setting, replete with angels, demon, spirits, and gods; others picture the hero on a landscape more familiar to our own common sense. No matter. The setting is, in a way, a question of time and taste. A modern Oedipus may well defeat a less fantastic riddler than the Sphinx and remain Oedipus still. To be sure, many of the characters who inhabit the cosmos of ancient mythology remind us of aspects of existence to which we tend to be blind and hence ought not to be dismissed as trivial. Surely the Bible would be poorer without Gabriel, Satan, the Cherubim, and the Lamb of God seated upon his throne. At the same time, we must shake ourselves loose from the idea that myths are designed primarily to teach the existence of such extraordinary characters in order to see that even without them the story still could be told with power.

Whether the myth be set in Valhalla, Middle Earth, or Hohokus, N.J., the ultimate backdrop of the myth is unspeakable. The hero moves toward victory through power obviously not his own. Helpers appear at exactly the right instant; his strength is renewed just as it seems ready to fail; events outside his control occur propitiously, if not miraculously. His triumph, then, is the triumph, not of himself, but of the Other. Yet of the unknown the myth does not, should not, can not speak univocally. To venture into the why of the victory too plainly would be to speak the unspeakable and hence to corrupt it.

This is the reason why the Gospel of John is so daringly dangerous, for in the hymnic prologue to the Gospel the author comes very close to objectifying and hence desecrating that which can never be an object.[2] Unlike the other gospels John is not satisfied only to relate the story of the saviour-hero; he feels compelled over and over again to remind the reader of that Unknown Light which Yeshua reveals and is.

As great a danger as this may be, it is also an essential danger to risk, lest the myth be read incorrectly. As long as we remember that this gospel begins with the words "In the beginning"—or, as might be more accurate, "Once upon a time"—we shall not badly err. Essentially, what John does is to describe the present analogically by projecting it backward to the beginning." He speaks of the now as though it were remotely then.

> In the beginning was the Word, and the Word was with God, And the Word was God. He was in the beginning with God; all things were made through him, and without him was not anything made that was made. In him was life, and the life was the light of men. The light shines in the darkness, and the darkness has not overcome it.
>
> There was a man sent from God, whose name was John. He came for testimony, to bear witness to the light, that all might believe through Him. He was not the light, but came to bear witness to the light.
>
> The true light that enlightens every man was coming into the world. He was in the world, and the world was made through him, yet the world knew him not. He came to his own home, and his own people received him not. But to all who received him, who believed in his name, he gave power to become children of God; who were born, not of blood nor of the will of the flesh nor of the will of man, but of God.
>
> And the Word became flesh and dwelt among us,

full of grace and truth; we have beheld his glory, glory
as of the only Son from the Father.

John 1:1-14

Once upon a time—at root—in the beginning was the Word.
LOGOS (Word has been and can be understood in a great variety
of ways but it is not our task here to sort through all the various
interpretations which have been given. Essentially, it is enough
to say that *Logos* is self-expression; it is the way by which what is
inward can be made outward. Humanly speaking, all words are
miraculous, for to turn an idea into a sound which others can
again translate into their own ideas is a transmogrification too
subtle to comprehend fully. Such a wonder, says John, is the very
root of the world. *Theos* speaks for himself, to himself,[3] and in so
doing brings the cosmos into existence. There is no "material"
substance set over against the "supernatural" substance of *Theos*,
for there is neither natural nor supernatural. The world, pro-
duced by God's speech, is what we know of the unknown. Logos
and Cosmos are inseparable.

This *Logos* of which John speaks not only was once the power of
creation at the beginning but performs this task at every instant.
The Logos is the animating and illuminating power of life. In so
far as humans are alive and conscious, they are so through the
Logos. It is not that the Word *ought* to illumine and activate
mankind. The Word *is* the illuminator and mover. The Word *is*
the light and life of man and the cosmos.

If a very mechanical and technological illustration may be per-
mitted, let us think of ourselves as watching a movie. This movie,
however, is not merely on a screen which occupies but a portion
of our visual field. Rather, every perception, both inward and
outward, is a part of the film. In a word, the movie equals all
external and internal sensations, thoughts, and feelings—it is the
contents of consciousness.

Each of us identifies with an actor or actress on the screen; yet
each, at the same time, is vaguely transcendent and can watch
that actor play out his or her part.[4] Nevertheless, most of us are
thoroughly wrapped up with one of the persons in the drama and
see things through his eyes.

What few see, however, is that there is, behind all the characters, but one light which animates them all. All depends upon that one projecting light; all is that one light. In effect, the characters, though apparently individual and sometimes at odds, are actually one. This one light is, of course, incomprehensible except by the wildest analogies, for all words are designed to describe things on the screen and the light is no one thing among many. Nevertheless, nothing could be known or spoken of, nothing would exist without that light, that source of existence.[5]

There was a man sent from God . . .

Suddenly upon the screen appears a new character, a man called John, who comes to point, not in any human direction, but to the light. He comes as a witness (*martyrion*) to that eternal light which is from the beginning and which, in a most unaccountable way, is now travelling incognito in the world. He comes to indicate the Word made flesh.

In one sense the Word is always becoming flesh, for the Word is the light which enlightens every man. The cosmos, that movie in which we are all engrossed, would not exist if that light did not shine. The Word which camps near us incognito, however, is of a special sort.

One is reminded of that age-old story of the Prince who searched most of his life for a pearl of great price, a precious gem for which all should be sold. He travelled the world over without success, seeking everywhere for that fabulous, elusive rarity. Finally, broken, ragged, and old he returned home empty-handed. As he knelt before a pool to drink, however, he saw that for which he had searched so long. It was the pearl—in the center of his forehead.

The Word incognito is like that reflecting pool. The Word comes into the world to reveal what man already is but doesn't recognize—the light which eternally shines. The mirror called the Word made flesh reveals that that ego which we have been trying so anxiously to protect and preserve is a piece of illusion which can never be secured. Inevitably, the ego will disappear; it is but one more character in the film which plays before us. Come life or come death, however, the light will continue to shine and we are all one in that light. The Word made flesh teaches us to refocus our eyes so that we see in ourselves and others not the shadows of darkness but the light of lights.

Needless to say, such refocusing is not merely an intellectual matter. Many people who know perfectly well that a movie is just a movie become emotionally overwrought when they actually sit in a darkened theatre engrossed in the drama before them. So too, even those who intellectually know better become so tied up with one character on the screen that only the darkness is seen.

Apprehension of the light is, in fact, not a matter of knowledge or experience at all, for all forms of knowledge and experience presuppose objects and the light is no object. If anything, the result of what has been called revelation is not-knowing, not-sensing, not-experiencing. It is not grasping but letting go, not flailing but floating. How, more precisely, one arrives at such an apprehension and learns to relax the grip on the ego is a question which we must examine much more fully as we proceed.

Lest there be misunderstanding at this point, it must be underlined that the recognition of the light as the light of the world and the consequent sense of ultimate unity by no means implies that the "film" being observed is of no interest or worth. On the contrary, that flickering projection called the cosmos arises through the Word by *Theos*.[6] What the revelation implies, however, is that we no longer need to be defensive about our projected egos but can take a much more relaxed and compassionate stance in life. Far from leading to hermitic detachment from others, the Word provides the basis for a new sense of profound unity with others. At root, all men are the light.

On the film which we are viewing, however, there is little unity but much alienation. In so far as there is love, it is *eros*, for humanity, far from celebrating its oneness, searches madly and vainly for security. Erotic love constitutes that search. The ego as such sees itself as but a minute fragment of the cosmos, beset on all sides by dangers and threats. Hence it is driven by both conscious and unconscious impulses to find the security it thinks it lacks.

The scenarios for the expression of such eros are infinitely varied and yet remarkably similar. Basically, eros either reaches out to control and dominate or to be controlled and dominated. Eros is the driving force behind both Master and Slave, both the sadist and the masochist. Domination and submission are but two sides of the same coin. From the point of view of this world, the happiest condition is found when such complementary opposites are coordinated.

Erotic love is usually thought of as sexual and so, in a limited sense, it is. The bedroom is frequently the stage where the quest for dominance and/or submissiveness is realized. Nevertheless, eros is equally present in the business office, the Senate cloak room, and even the classroom. In fact, eros so motivates human existence that there is scarcely an instant that passes when it is not expressed in some way.

Religious thought and action also can be highly erotic in nature. That is, the individual in religion submits, not to another person (though that is possible too) but to a supernatural force which is conceived to be a part of, and yet to transcend the cosmic drama and who, in receiving the submission of erotic love, grants in return the security of his power. Many gods of this sort even promise immortality to the ego which exhibits really submissive behavior. In some quarters the willingness to believe the most ridiculous and contradictory assertions counts very heavily in favor of the self, for it suggests extraordinary submission.[7]

The problem is, however, that no matter how fervent the eros is there is no ultimate security for the ego. The ego is ephemeral and finite; it is subject to extinction in death. Therefore, the more security the ego seeks for, the more frantic the quest becomes. In every instance, the sought-for security eludes the lover. The Master, if he is honest, finds that he is nothing without the Slave. The Slave, in turn, is driven to new insecurities by the limited nature of his Master's power. The seduced and the seducer need each other and yet each finds the other less than wholly fulfilling. Even the bride of God discovers that the concept submitted to is just that—a concept. Only the most cleverly imposed blinders can prevent that resurgence of the insecurity which is feared so much. No amount of grasping, clinging, or submitting can prevent the ultimate destruction of that one character we all love (and covertly hate); our Ego.

In so far as religion expresses man's erotic quest, it is a part of the cosmic dance of illusion. It may be comic or tragic, depending upon one's point of view, but it is not salvific. Even the profoundest act of submission to God is but one more attempt to prevent the inevitable: the destruction of the ego. This is the reason why religion can be so dangerous. Frequently, it is a means through which the ego, now submissive to God, becomes so inflated with the power of God that the bravado of the ego knows no bounds. Religion becomes the source and buttress for the most vicious and pervasive forms of egotism.

Therefore, those theologies which point to man's varied erotic quests for security as somehow intimations and hints of what man's true quest should be are quite dangerously wrong. If "concern" is to be found in man's erotic attempts to prop up the ego, ultimate security will not be found in some Ultimate Concern, for concern is at root egotistical.[8] There is no continuity between erotic love and what the New Testament terms *agape*.

It is dangerous even to speak about *agape* for any description is likely to be misunderstood. Perhaps the best approach is to define *agape* negatively. Although both *eros* and *agape* are translated "love," *agape* is the obverse of *eros*. *Agape* does not grasp for security but lets it go. *Agape* is to *eros* as the opening of the hand is to its closing.

Eros is evident in every aspect of human existence, for the ego is the offspring and ward of *eros*. *Agape*, on the other hand, can never be recognized or proved; *agape* travels incognito. This is particularly true in the realm of religion where *eros* is often so much in evidence. *Agrape* is never directed to God or any other so-called supernatural being.[9] Nevertheless, he who is enlightened finds *agae* welling up like water from a spring of living water. He who walks in the light *agapes* the cosmos.[10]

"The world knew him not . . . "

The Word appears with radiance in the world; yet many do not recognize the *logos* glory. The children of darkness see but another character on the stage of life, a character who hardly seems satisfactory as an object of religious (erotic) love. How, after all, could such a man grant security? How could such a threatening and forbidding figure bring peace?

True, there are those who try to transform Yeshua into one who will provide the security for which our egos search. Like Mary of Magdala on the morning of the resurrection they wish to grab hold of him as the major prop and support in life. But Yeshua eludes the grasp. He pries the fingers loose and sends all away empty-handed. He will not allow himself to become an ally of the old Adam. Those who wish to save themselves are told that the ego must be lost, destroyed, crucified.

There are those, however, who do see and believe. See what? Believe what? Nothing. Or rather they see precisely what the children of darkness see: a prophet, a wonder worker, a teacher. And yet—this is the paradoxical part—they know themselves to be one with him "who was born not out of human stock or urge of the flesh or will of man but of God himself." (1:13) The eyes see nothing new but are refocused to apprehend the one light rather than the darkness.

The Word for them becomes no new object for erotic piety or cultic devotion. The light is no thing which can be separated out for special reverence from other things. Yeshua is Adam. The light is everything and yet no thing. In this sense, there is no distinction between the children of light and the children of darkness.

Still, for the children of light that cord of erotic craving is severed. The search for salvation is over. The drowning man who thrashed this way and that now floats upon his back quietly. The ego may be washed away at floodtide but the light will continue to shine. It is as though the beginning is now. God says, "Let there be light, and there is light." (Gen. 1:3)

Suddenly, the celluloid cosmos which once seemed so solid and real and permanent begins to turn up at the corners as the searing light ignites it. Time, which appeared so immensely long and ponderous, collapses into a fraction of a fraction of an instant. Even the most venerable teachers—like Moses—appear to be but unworthy supporters of the old ego. To be sure, the Law teaches man the rudiments of ego-control; its commandments and prohibitions curtail some of the worst abuses of eroticism. But in the end, ego-control turns out to be but a new form of egotism. The most fastidious followers of the Law, the Pharisees, are also furthest from the truth.

Yeshua reveals, not ego-control, but ego-crucifixion, not a new Decalogue but grace and truth. The way of Yeshua is no new Law or doctrine or life-style. His way is no way; what he reveals is no thing. *Theos* can not be seen because *Theos* cannot be objectified. We can only speak mythologically: just as a son reflects the form of the father (for he is shaped by his genes), so Yeshua reveals the no thingness from which he springs and in which we are all rooted. The truth he brings is the precise opposite of facts. Facts are finished, past, objectified, and dead. Truth is open, present, nothing, and alive.

As was said at the beginning of this chapter, such an exposition of the Christian myth as has been given may be necessary, but it is also highly dangerous. Particularly risky is the image of the film which pictures God as here and the cosmos as a projection "over there," for this is to transform *Theos* into an object and not even a very elegant object at that.

Hence, it is very important that we now erase what has been said and pronounce all our analogies wanting. There is no "something" which stands over against the world and creates it. *Theos* is neither a celestial lamp nor a cosmic spring. In so far as the Word reveals at all, it reveals no thing. In a sense, all of our analogies and vain linguistic gropings are designed to say precisely that. Ultimate wisdom is silence. Theology is a task which involves writing with one hand and erasing simultaneously with the other. Between the creation of the right hand and the destruction of the left there should be no temporal interval at all.

3

WATER AND WIND

In those days came John the Baptist, preaching in the wilderness of Judea, "Repent, for the kingdom of heaven is at hand." For this is he who was spoken of by the prophet Isaiah when he said,
> The voice of one crying in the wilderness:
> Prepare the way of the LORD
> make his paths straight.

Now John wore a garment of camel's hair, and a leather girdle around his waist; and his food was locusts and wild honey. Then went out to him Jerusalem and all Judea and all the region about the Jordan, and they were baptized by him in the river Jordan confessing their sins.

But when he saw many of the Pharisees and Sadducees coming for baptism, he said to them, "You brood of vipers. Who warned you to flee from the wrath to come? Bear fruit that befits repentance, and do not presume to say to yourselves, 'We have Abraham as our father'; for I tell you, God is able from these stones to raise up children to Abraham. Even now the axe is laid to the root of the trees; every tree therefore that does not bear good fruit is cut down and thrown into the fire.

"I baptize you with water for repentance, but he who is coming after me is mightier than I, whose sandals I am not worthy to carry; he will baptize you with the Holy Spirit and with fire. His winnowing fork is in his hand, and he will clear his threshing floor and gather his wheat into the granary, but the chaff he will burn with unquenchable fire."

Then Jesus came from Galilee to the Jordan to John, to be baptized by him. John would have prevented him, saying, "I need to be baptized by you, and do you come to me?" But Jesus answered him, "Let it be so now; for thus it is fitting for us to fulfill all righteousness" Then he consented. And when Jesus was baptized, he went up immediately from the water, and behold, the heavens were opened and he saw the Spirit of God descending like a dove, and alighting on him; and lo, a voice from heaven saying, "This is my beloved Son, with whom I am well-pleased."

Matt. 3:1-17

T he story of the Flood, that deluge which cleanses the earth and brings to man both death and rebirth, is one of the most universal myths known to mankind.[1] Nearly every culture has retold the story from its own perspective so that a great variety of reasons for and results of the disaster has been given. Still, the mythic remembrance of devastating waters rising over the earth seems to be worldwide.

For the Jew, quite typically, the reason for the Flood and for every other human disaster patterned after it, is sin.[2] Man disobeys God and becomes corrupt; his evil imagination leads to violence and perversity. Repentance is called for but man refuses. Hence, God sends destruction upon the earth to cleanse man of his unrighteousness and to produce a new heaven and a new earth. In the midst of this apparent chaos one man is chosen for all. Noah rides out the flood waters of disaster and eventually initiates a new age. The old, corrupt man is destroyed but the new man is preserved.

The baptism of John is a simulation of that cataclysm and rebirth. To be immersed by him is to repent of the past, to undergo death in the flood waters of destruction, and to arise, ready for the new kingdom at hand. By undergoing this rite in the Jordan River, men prepare themselves for the wrath to come and gain confidence in the day of hope beyond disaster.

By wearing camel skins and living the life of a desert ascetic, John acts out the part of Elijah, that prophet who, according to Malachi 4:5, will return before the great and terrible day of the

Lord. He is not the one who will begin the revolution itself; he makes no claim to Messiahship. Rather he prepares the way in the wilderness beyond the Jordan, waiting for him who will baptize with Holy Spirit and fire.

John's message, as it is recorded in the Gospel of Matthew, is brief and yet filled with extraordinarily powerful images. Basically he makes three important points:

First, John proclaims the imminent arrival of the reign of Heaven (i.e., God)[3] and calls his hearers to repentance METANOIA. Such repentance is not just feeling sorry for past sins and promising to lead a new life. Repentance means turning around and going in the opposite direction. It means walking on that straight path which John prepares in the wilderness.

Second, the radical nature of this about face is demonstrated in his works to the Pharisees and Sadducees. Not only the people of the land but religious leaders as well come to hear John and perhaps even seek baptism. One might expect him to be pleased by the interest accorded him by those in authority, but he is not. These pious, holy men he pictures as like a nest of poisonous snakes slithering out of the grass to escape the fiery wrath which is overtaking them. Who clued you in about the coming wrath? he asks.[4]

The question is, why are these men pictured as so despicable? What is their crime? Significantly, John does not attack either their religious commitment or their moral scrupulosity in the Gospel of Matthew. Rather, he vilifies them because they claim Abraham as their father.

> Do not presume to say to yourselves, 'We have Abraham as our father'; for I tell you, God is able from these stones to raise up children to Abraham.
>
> Matt. 3:9

At first, such an attack seems peculiar, for one of the central emphases of Judaism was and is its lineal descent from the "father of a multitude." Why should John single out this claim for special condemnation? Why shouldn't a Jew claim Abraham as his father?

Just as the chief danger of the individual is to be deluded by that self-creation called the ego, so the great danger of religion and society is to forsake the living present for the dead, past, corporate ego. Indeed, concern for the perpetuation of tradition is usually but a projection of ego illusion upon a larger screen. As a result, faith is replaced by belief, freedom by the bondage of convention, truth, by fact. This is precisely that from which John calls men to turn. The age of a fruit tree means nothing to the arboriculturalist; what matters is the fruit it bears. If the tree does not bear well, it must be cut down to make room for a more productive tree. One of the great dangers of religion in particular is that it concentrates all too frequently upon the antiquity of the tree rather than upon its fruit.

John recognizes the power of traditional religion's message. Identification with ancient tradition seems to provide the security for which many yearn. The preacher, however, reminds his hearers (and us) that even the most ancient traditions will die if they lack the vital power of faith. Right now, he says, the owner of the orchard is inspecting and marking his trees. Soon, he will be chopping down all those which are past bearing. The fruit which Abraham once bore is of no interest today. The question is: how good is the fruit now? With that question in mind, John calls men from reliance upon the security of tradition to enter the kingdom of heaven.

Third, John teaches that the kingdom is fast approaching and that one endowed with great power and stature will soon arrive to effect the transformation which he, John, heralds. He has no qualms attacking both civil and religious authorities—in fact he is arrested and executed for his audacity—but he sees himself as nothing compared to the one who is to come.

> He will baptize you with the Holy Spirit and fire.
>
> Matt. 3:11

By way of explanation, John pictures a winnower on his threshing floor with his shovel in his hand. First, he throws the unwinnowed grain in the air, allowing the wind to blow the chaff to one side. After the wind has done its work and the kernels of wheat alone are left by his feet, the winnower burns the chaff with fire.

This is the way the mighty one who is to come will work. He will so shake society that the Holy Spirit (*Pneuma* means either spirit or wind) can test each person (and society as a whole), separating wheat and chaff.[5] The worthless outer husk (what we might interpret as the old ego) will be burned up and destroyed while the inner core, the kernel, (i.e., the eternal light) will be saved. Baptism prepares the faithful for this winnowing process by turning men from their outward, personal and corporate egos to the unspeakable present.

When Yeshua arrives from Galilee, John immediately recognizes him as the One whom he heralds and hence hesitates to baptize him. Yeshua, however, insists "for the sake of righteousness," and John, in the end, complies. The ego of Yeshua, like the ego of each one of us, must be washed off. Otherwise he will become only a cultic idol, an object for eros, and not a revelation of truth. Yeshua is to be distinguished from other men, not because his ego is better but because it is dissolved. Yeshua is Everyman and hence must die and rise again from a watery grave. At the beginning of his ministry, he sets out his whole epic journey. The old Adam, the old age, the old dispensation are plunged into the river and from the water emerges a new reality. Not new in a temporal sense. "Before Abraham was, I am," says Yeshua.[6] New in the sense of being present not past, living not dead, light not darkness.

At this instant, the heavens are opened, a fissure rends the cosmos, and we perceive the principal, hidden characters in the drama. Usually, commentators interpret this and other similar passages symbolically, but we must remind ourselves that the myth itself makes no clear distinctions between historical and symbolical passages. The reader cannot insist upon the historical nature of the story and then, when it suits his fancy, forsake the historical for the symbolic. If the baptism of Jesus is to be regarded as historical then the dove, the rending of heaven and the Father's voice are historical too. Within the context of the story we have the reporting of actual visual and auditory sensations, the sensations of Yeshua himself. The dove is not introduced as a symbol for the Holy Spirit. Yeshua sees the Holy Spirit as a dove; He hears the Father as a voice from Heaven. Eventually, the dove became a symbol. At the start, however, it was the reality of the Spirit.

Here, in this juxtaposition of Father, Son, and Holy Spirit we find *in nuce* that hallmark of Christian understanding which outsiders are likely to regard as most peculiar, i.e., the Trinity. Its apparent peculiarity stems from the fact that most people begin by equating the Father in heaven with God and then proceed to wonder how Christ and the Holy Spirit can be God also. In truth, however, the myth directs us beyond the mistake of identifying one character in the story with *Theos* to see that all three divine participants in the drama point beyond themselves to the unutterable Godhead which transcends both the story and us. What looks at first like irrational foolishness is a mythic means of leading the reader beyond the worship of the Father as an idol.

Yeshua upon arising from the water is the kernel which remains when the old man has been blown or washed away: the chosen one, the elect, the Father's Son. He is the Beloved One,[7] that which undergirds the cosmos and whom the Father loves. Theologians of the Augustinian tradition in particular have, in the past, distinguished between those who are elect and those who are damned.[8] This is to misconstrue the meaning of the New Testament. *All* egos, as chaff, are bound for the flame; *all* men of the cosmos perish. In the Son, however, men find their life and light; he is *Adam*, man. Thus, at root all are secure.

At his baptism Yeshua is identified as the One light which shines forth from *Theos* and in whom all are saved. It is he who survives every baptism in the water of death. Salvation emerges from the water when one "believes into" that light.[9] Faith is neither simply accepting orthodox dogmas nor even trusting in a Supreme Being. "Faith into" means entering into and knowing oneself to be one with that realm of light.

In one sense, the message "Repent for the Kingdom of Heaven is at hand," was not new with either John or Jesus. Jews had entertained apocalyptic hopes for centuries and had looked forward to an anointed one (Messiah) who would drive out the foreign enemies, establish righteous rule in Israel, and usher in a new and durable age of peace.[10] John and Yeshua use common words but transform them into something extraordinarily uncommon. This is what makes the New Testament such enormously difficult series of texts to read. The old language is preserved but in a radically new sense. By the end of the book of Revelation scarcely one conceptual stone is left unturned.

41

For many apocalyptic Jews the destruction to come was to be historical and political.[11] And so was the hope. The forecast was for bloody turmoil, the end of the regime, and the initiation of the Messianic, but earthly kingdom. Yeshua preserves many of the images of this forecast but as parables of something much higher and deeper. The revolution is but an intimation of the destruction and reconstitution of the cosmos itself.

Repentance, for the Jew, was a moral act. It meant regret for past sins and a resolve to live a better, more righteous life. It meant return to Torah and oral law.[12] It meant a supreme effort to obey the commandments. Repentance for Yeshua, on the other hand, is not simply a matter of turning from immorality to either Jewish law or some other moral vision. Repentance rather means a frontal attack upon the chief of the culprits, the illusory but deceptive ego.

The task of repentance is not to get the ego to act more morally or religiously, for the moral ego is the ego still, the crafty and subtle deluder who inevitably brings man to despair. Yeshua calls upon man to crucify the ego and enter the kingdom. Repentance, then, is not a turning from this human path to that. It is not merely seeking to live a better life, following the commandments of the Heavenly Father. Repentance for Yeshua is total turning—from the cosmos to the light, from ego to "I am," from something to no thing.

Yeshua comes proclaiming the kingdom, but it is not the kingdom of David. "Kingdom of God" (like "Gospel," "New Adam," and "Faith") is a way of pointing to that eternal, unspeakable Suchness which is always presupposed but never known. The image of the Messianic kingdom, however, is used in parable form to point the way, for it emphasizes the ephemerality of the cosmos and life and the transcendent character of meaning. Yeshua speaks of the coming of the Kingdom precisely because such an image makes clear that the meaning of the drama we call history is not in the drama itself at all but in the intervening present which makes the past possible.

Yeshua's baptism is a dramatization on the screen of history of that miracle called repentance, an act which culminates in a voice from heaven saying, "You are my Son, the Beloved, with whom I am well-pleased." The inner, heavenly eye is opened, a dove descends from heaven and man's divine lineage is made plain. Yeshua remains a man, fully and wholly a man; yet his humanity is now transparent. The light of lights shines forth.

> Then Jesus was led up by the Spirit into the wilderness to be tempted by the devil. And he fasted forty days and forty nights, and afterward he was hungry. And the tempter came and said to him, "If you are the Son of God, command these stones to become loaves of bread." But he answered, "It is written,
> > 'Man shall not live by bread alone,
> > but by every word that proceeds from
> > the mouth of God.'"
> Then the devil took him to the holy city, and set him on the pinnacle of the temple, and said to him, "If you are the Son of God, throw yourself down; for it is written,
> > 'He will give his angels charge of you,
> > and
> > 'On their hands they will bear you up,
> > lest you strike your feet against a stone.'"
> Jesus said to him, "Again it is written. 'You shall not tempt the Lord your God.'" Again, the devil took him to a very high mountain, and showed him all the kingdoms of the world and the glory of them; and he said to him, "All these I will give you, if you will fall down and worship me." Then Jesus said to him, "Be-gone, Satan! for it is written,
> > 'You shall worship the Lord your God
> > and him only shall you serve.'"
> Then the devil left him, and behold, angels came and ministered to him.
>
> Matt. 4:1-11

Immediately after his baptism, Yeshua's realization is put to the test. Frequently, the above-quoted passage is called the temptation of Jesus, but that is a misnomer. It is the Spirit which drives him from the tropical lushness of the Jordan Valley into the sterile wilderness. It is the Spirit which arranges for the test which Yeshua must undergo. It is the Spirit which, as a winnow-ing wind, insures that only the kernel, only the now man is left.

Yeshua's examiner, however, is not the Spirit but the *Diabolé*, the Spirit's opposite and alter ego. *Diabolé*, the Greek equivalent of the Hebrew Satan, is often translated "devil" but that may be more misleading than helpful. Surely we ought not to think of *diabolé* as a sneering fellow with a red suit and a long, pointed tail. *Diabolé* means, in effect, he who throws up against—both in the sense of accusing and in the sense of deluding. His role is that of an examiner, to see whether Yeshua will fall prey to the illusions of the ego which he throws up or whether he can overcome that very human temptation to support and expand man's perennial fantasy.

Before the test begins, Yeshua prepares himself by fasting for forty days and forty nights. That is, he takes upon himself one of man's oldest and most effective religious disciplines. Because of lack of experience with such discipline, modern readers are likely to understand fasting as a repudiation or punishment of the flesh. Nothing, however, could be further from the case. Fasting, breath control, postures, and the like are not usually used by holy men to punish the body but dominate it. Fasting is a way of bringing the body under control so that truth from the depths can emerge. Deprivation clears the mind of ordinary thoughts, strengthens the will, and allows that landscape normally hidden from man in the depths of his own uncounscious to surface.[13]

At the same time, a long fast is extraordinarily taxing and leaves man, at the end, in a weakened and vulnerable state for which hunger is hardly a fully adequate expression. Just as the forty-day period ends, the accuser appears before Yeshua's eyes to attack what looks like his weakest spot.

"If you are the Son of God, command these stones to become loaves of bread." After forty days of fast, the thought of using "Kingdom power" to make bread surely must have been exceptionally attractive. But it also represents a test of the most subtle sort. Eating, of course, is necessary for life and Yeshua repeatedly acknowledges this. He is not an ascetic who believes that supplying the body's needs is evil.[14] Nevertheless, eating in quantity is not nearly so necessary as most of us imagine. In fact, eating functions frequently as a way of attempting to expand and secure the ego. Hence, insecurity is likely to foster the worst sorts of overindulgence. As usual, man's evil imagination corrupts the body by turning legitimate hunger into one more search for security for the ego.

Human beings, it would seem, often take into themselves the fruits of earth with the unconscious or semi-conscious aim of making themselves more palpable and real. Or, since there are limits to the amount one can eat, many surround themselves with things in abundance. Man becomes a consumer, hoping thereby to find security. Things are used to enlarge the ego and to make it appear important before other men.

Exactly the opposite, of course, occurs. The more one eats, the more insecure one becomes. Obesity does not save but only endangers. The acquisition of too many unneeded things is but another form of obesity which is equally debilitating. Not only are mink stoles ruined by moths and Cadillacs by rust but the more affluence one "enjoys" the more thieves and robbers become a danger.[15] Basically "goods" are not well named, for they bring as much insecurity as security. Invariably a philosophy of affluence and the threat of crime go hand in hand. The more men seek security in things, the more others aim to take away that security by poser or stealth. Hence, even under deprived conditions, Yeshua resists the possibility of using his power to turn stones into bread, either for himself or for anyone else. Yeshua attacks, not the threat of starvation, but the real enemy of man—the illusory ego which constantly blinds man, turning him into a ravenous consumer.

This is not to say that the things of this world are themselves evil. On the contrary, it is not the world but man's erotic imagination which is evil. What is destructive is the quest for security which possessiveness represents. The illumined one may own property and enjoy the good things of life—Yeshua himself seems to have owned a house in Capernaum[16]—but he must beware the egoistic illusions which present the loss of property as the loss of self. Hence, property must be dealt with cavalierly. If someone asks for something, give it away![17] Don't hang on to things as though your life depends upon them. Take the middle path between the ascetic rejection of, and the erotic hunger for the world.[18]

The second test is, in a way, a more refined version of the first, for the search for adulation and praise is but a less tangible form of consumerism. In effect, the deluder suggests that Yeshua "show off" by jumping from the pinnacle of the Temple. Such a miracle, he implies, will be likely to win many admirers and will bolster Yeshua's cause.

Yeshua, however, will have nothing to do with such public relations stunts, for he is not at all interested in attracting admirers. His aim is not to impress people but to call them into the Kingdom by opening their inner eye to the light.[19] Were he to care about proving himself before others or receiving their praise he would show himself to be totally unillumined.

In truth, the quest for security through public admiration can only lead to greater and greater insecurity. The magician must do harder and harder tricks to keep his audience. If he does not, they will soon yawn and turn away. Audiences are looking for their own security. They want to be able to brag that they have seen something new and exciting. This means that the performer must constantly work to please. The admired becomes totally dependent upon and the servant of those who admire. Ultimately, this leads to the profoundest forms of insecurity.

Yeshua does not reject magic as a part of his ministry but uses his powers where they are needed. He does not retreat to the hills as a solitary hermit but remains constantly in the public eye. His life therefore is an example of that narrow middle path which neither rejects society nor depends upon the admiration of society.

The final test goes one step further as the deluder suggests that Yeshua gain power over the whole world through the worship of the devil. The Enlightened One, however, sees that the search for security through power is but an inverted form of the quest for security through admiration. Just as the admired one is defined by the admirers so the Master is defined by his slaves.

The worship of one's own ego may lead to power over the world—or at least some piece of it—but it is always a power which is balanced by powerlessness. The most insecure, captive persons in the world are the tyrants, for behind every hedge and wall lurks an assassin's bullet. Just as "consumerism" breeds crime and "admirationism," contempt, so the quest for power fosters revolution and social chaos. Had Yeshua succumbed to the *Diabolé*, he would have become the devil himself.

Once more, Yeshua's rejection of this temptation does not mean his rejection of civil authority. He is perfectly willing to render to Caesar the things which are Caesar's[20]; despite the horrible political conditions of the time his teaching is not that of an anarchist or even a revolutionary of the usual sort. What he considers dangerous is not government or civil law or even political power; it is the corruption of these things by man's evil imagination.

Unlike most of us Yeshua passes the deluder's test because he is fully aware that the ego offers no security at all and therefore that there is no point in buttressing that dead figment of man's imagination. He perceives that it is the ego which is the primary cause of man's insecurity in the first place. We see the ego upon the screen and begin to worry about all the apparent forces which stand against it. Within the cosmic framework, the ego appears so small that it seems all too easy to destroy it. Yeshua calls us to abandon all these futile attempts to secure the old man and to turn our eyes instead to the one true light which is the source of all being. "For whoever would save his life will lose it, but he who loses his life for my sake and the gospel's will save it."

Mark 8:35

4

THE WAY

O nce illumined and tested the hero returns with a boon for mankind. He chooses disciples and becomes a teacher of wisdom. Whether he instructs his disciples in secret or addresses crowds openly, however, his task is not easy, for no words can describe the Unknown Beyond to which he has crossed and from which he now returns. He must speak the language of the old man, even when he instructs his disciples privately. He can, perhaps, point out the fruits of wisdom in the lives of the blessed and indicate the distinction between the illumined disciple and the man of the cosmos, but of the root of illumination he can only speak with the greatest circumspection. Even analogies are dangerous for they are easily transformed in to dogmas. At best the hero seeks to dissolve the common sense tenets of the age so that light begins to break forth.

I. The Blessed

Seeing the crowds, he went up on the mountain, and when he sat down his disciples came to him. And he opened his mouth and taught them, saying:

Blessed are the poor in spirit, for theirs is the kingdom of heaven.

Blessed are those who mourn, for they shall be comforted.

Blessed are the meek, for they shall inherit the earth.

Blessed are those who hunger and thirst for righteousness, for they shall be satisfied.

Blessed are the merciful, for they shall obtain mercy.

Blessed are the pure in heart, for they shall see God.

Blessed are the peacemakers, for they shall be called sons of God.

Blessed are those who are persecuted for righteousness' sake, for theirs is the kingdom of heaven.

Blessed are you when men revile you and persecute you and utter all kinds of evil against you falsely on my account. Rejoice and be glad, for your reward is great in heaven, for so men persecuted the prophets who were before you.

Matt. 5:12

Despite the supposed impact of Christianity upon Western culture, most of us implicitly accept that old Epicurean notion that pleasure is good and pain is evil. Hence, people of means who enjoy the many things which affluence brings are thought of as happy while beggars, lamenters, and those hounded and pursued by the law certainly are not. What, after all, could be more piteous than a bereaved wife wailing over the coffin of a husband killed in action or a fugitive fleeing desperately from a tyrant's police and blood hounds? So entrenched are our opinions that we can scarcely hear what Yeshua is saying in this first portion of what has been traditionally called the Sermon on the Mount.[1]

What, in effect, he does is to turn our whole world topsy-turvy by commending to us both attitudes and conditions radically foreign to our common sense. We rub our eyes in amazement and disbelief as he identifies some of the ugliest and most threatening possibilities of human existence as supremely blessed. In other places he casts a critical, even condemnatory eye upon the rich; here Yeshua seems to glorify a life of poverty.

To be sure, he does say, "Blessed are the poor *in spirit*" (but Cf. the parallel in Luke 6:20). No such qualification, however, is given for the commendation of the mourners or those being persecuted. What is it that someone who wails has which a rich man in his comfort does not? What is it about being a beggar,[2] either in fact or in spirit (whatever that might mean) which ought to be emulated? How can Yeshua call the poor, the insignificant, and the powerless happy?

We return once more to our central point: As long as a person is deluded by the old man, the ego, and identifies himself with that dead fantasy, riches, influence, and power will appear as the greatest goods on earth, for they seem to promise security against disaster. They are ways of keeping the old man alive and propped up as long as possible.

Once that illusion is dissolved by the intense radiance of the Light, however, those same goods appear as the most grievous albatross around the neck. Affluence provides neither happiness nor security but often exactly the reverse. If the cord of desire is not snapped, only bondage and death are the result. Hence it is as difficult for a rich man to enter the kingdom of heaven as for a camel to pass through the eye of a needle (Mark 10:25; Matt. 19:24; Luke 18:25). This is the reason why Yeshua tells the rich young man to sell all he has and follow him.[3]

The opposite of the bondage of affluence, however, is not simple poverty, for the poor man may be just as bound by desire as he who is rich and may believe that his basic need is wealth, not revelation. Hence Yeshua does not unambiguously teach that the rich are bad and the poor good. Rather, it is the beggars in spirit and those who are persecuted in the cause of right who are already in the Kingdom. Meekness, mourning, feeling famished for the right, mercy, purity of heart, and peace-making are signs that the cord of desire is snapping and that the light will dawn, but the full reality is not yet here.

These promises of Yeshua—that, for instance, those who mourn shall be comforted—raise a whole new set of questions. How can he make such bold and unaccountable assertions? In what sense will the mourners be comforted and the meek inherit the earth? Jesus employs here the apocalyptic language of his time—the day will come when these wrongs will be righted—but it is also obvious that he does not think of the coming of the Kingdom in a wholly temporal sense. Otherwise, the Kingdom of Heaven would not already be the "property" of the spiritual beggars.

Rather, he seems to be implying that the blows which reign upon the head of the outward man and the good acts which that man does have a profound compensatory effect upon the inner, hidden, new Adam. Or rather, more precisely, effects of the present upon the old man reveal themselves in mercy, justice, and peace which, in turn, serve as signs for the Kingdom. In the cosmos men may look for things and never find them but in the world of light all who seek find. The merciful shall receive mercy, the man whose heart has been purified shall see God. The Heavenly Father is not a divine potentate who chooses by whim. In the realm of the Kingdom "he who works will get the bread."

Some interpreters have taken Yeshua's remarks about riches and poverty as "counsels of perfection" which can be followed only by the few, i.e., by the monastics, but not by the "ordinary" Christian.[4] Others have seen these statements as ways of inducing in all men a sense of sin and need for forgiveness.[5] Both these points of view are partially correct but basically misleading. Surely Yeshua does see that only a few will be able to follow the straight and narrow path which he lays out; he also is repeatedly intent upon awakening men to the fact of their own blindness (sin). There are few indications, however, that Yeshua distinguished between ordinary and super Christians or that he believed remorse for sin enough.

Yeshua comes as light in the darkness. He comes to open the inner eye to that light, to snap like tow the bonds of desire which bind men to the cosmos, and to drown eros in that living water called agape which bubbles up to eternity. He is not interested in building an organization which will appeal to or encompass all types of men; he does not offer a message attractive to the common sense of the usual political leader, ecclesiastical manipulator, or industrial giant. His word, like a sword, cuts to the bone. You cannot serve both God and Mammon. You must rid yourself of the illusions of the flesh and the ego. You must crucify yourself if you are to gain salvation. Crucifixion is not a counsel of perfection; it is the one event which makes the difference.

II. Salt and Light

You are the salt of the earth; but if the salt has lost its taste, how shall its saltness be restored? It is no longer good for anything except to be thrown out and trodden under foot by men.

You are the light of the world. A city set on a hill cannot be hid. Nor do men light a lamp and put it

under a bushel, but on a stand, and it gives light to all
in the house. Let your light so shine before men, that
they may see your good works and give glory to your
Father who is in heaven.

Matt. 5:13-16

In this second, short section Yeshua expresses, among other
things, his rationale for concern about action in the world. Why,
if the cosmos is largely a product of man's imagination and an
endless illustration of his bondage in eros should the enlightened
one be concerned about it? Why should the man of faith, he who
has crossed to the other side on the great ship called REPENTANCE,
care about the illusory cosmos at all? Should not the illumined go
into hiding until the end of the last reel?

Yeshua answers these questions in two ways. First, it is the
illumined one and only he who can keep the cosmos from becoming absolutely banal and chaotic. Just as salt gives food its flavor,
so the enlightened provide those hints of light and purpose
which keep the whole drama of life from becoming meaningless
babble. Without the one who walks in the light, the cosmos
would become meaningless, hateful nonsense.

Second, the enlightened ones are, in fact, the light of the
world;[6] they are at root that reality which is called by John Logos.
As such they can serve as guiding lamps for other men so that
they too can find the Way. To hide that light is to misuse it.
Illumination is not given to support the ego but to radiate in the
cosmos before men so that they may also cross the great divide
and leave eros for agape. To light a lamp and put it under a bushel
is to waste the light which might otherwise illumine the Way.

Clearly Yeshua does not believe that the illumined stay in the
world to improve or perfect it. The cosmos will always remain the
dead and lifeless arena in which egos search erotically for security. Nothing can save the cosmos as such except destruction.
Nothing can save the egos of the cosmos except annihilation.
Nevertheless, the illumined can help to radiate light in the world
of darkness, reveal the light which the darkness hides, and restore the unity of the light which the cosmos refracts.

III. The Law

Think not that I have come to abolish the law and the prophets; I have come not to abolish them but to fulfill them. For truly, I say to you, till heaven and earth pass away, not an iota, not a dot, will pass from the law until all is accomplished. Whoever then relaxes one of the least of these commandments and teaches men so, shall be called least in the kingdom of heaven; but he who does them and teaches them shall be called great in the kingdom of heaven. For I tell you, unless your righteousness exceeds that of the scribes and Pharisees, you will never enter the kingdom of heaven.

You have heard that it was said to the men of old, "You shall not kill; and whoever kills shall be liable to judgment." But I say to you that every one who is angry with his brother shall be liable to judgment; whoever insults his brother shall be liable to council, and whoever says, "You fool!" shall be liable to the hell of fire. So if you are offering your gift there before the altar and there remember that your brother has something against you, leave your gift there before the altar and go; first be reconciled to your brother, and then come and offer your gift. Make friends quickly with your accuser, while you are going with him to court, lest your accuser hand you over to the judge, and the judge to the guard, and you be put in prison; truly, I say to you, you will never get out till you have paid the last penny.

You have heard that it was said, "You shall not commit adultery." But I say to you that every one who looks at a woman lustfully has already committed adultery with her in his heart. If your right eye causes you to sin, pluck it out and throw it away; it is better that you lose one of your members than that your whole body be thrown into hell. And if your right hand causes you to sin, cut it off and throw it away; it is better that you lose one of your members than that your whole body go into hell. It was also said, "Whoever divorces his wife, let him give a certificate of divorce." But I say to you that every one who divorces his wife, except on the ground of unchastity, makes her an adulteress; and whoever marries a divorced woman commits adultery.

Again you have heard that it was said to the men of old, "You shall not swear falsely, but shall perform to the Lord what you have sworn." But I say to you, Do not swear at all, either by heaven, for it is the throne of God or by the earth, for it is his footstool, or by Jerusalem, for it is the city of the great King. And do not swear by your head, for you cannot make one hair white or black. Let what you say be simply "Yes" or "No"; anything more than this comes from evil.

You have heard that it was said, "An eye for an eye and a tooth for a tooth." But I say to you, Do not resist one who is evil, But if any one strikes you on the right cheek, turn to him the other also; and if any one would sue you and take your coat, let him have your cloak as well; and if any one forces you to go one mile, go with him two miles. Give to him who begs from you, and do not refuse him who would borrow from you.

You have heard that it was said, "You shall love your neighbor and hate your enemy." But I say to you, Love your enemies and pray for those who persecute you, so that you may be sons of your Father who is in heaven; for he makes his sun rise on the evil and the good, and sends rain on the just and on the unjust. For if you love those who love you, what reward have you? Do not even the tax collectors do the same? And if you salute only your brethren, what more are you doing than others? Do not even the Gentiles do the same? You, therefore, must be perfect, as your heavenly Father is perfect.

Matt. 5:17-48

What is the relation between the illuminating light which Yeshua reflects and is and traditional Jewish law? What connection is there between the light of the world and the moral forms and tendencies of human culture and religion? Is there any direct link between illumination and commandment?

Yeshua makes clear at the outset that he does not intend to provide a new and higher moral or civil law. He is not a law giver like Moses nor does he want to tinker with the given law to improve it. Clearly, what the world needs is not a new and improved form of law but the light toward which the Law and the Prophets point. To relax the Law would only be to dissolve those restraints which those before us saw as necessary to control the most vicious forms of egotism. To be sure, the Law and the Prophets do not, can not dissolve the ego; traditional religion itself often represents egotism in its most blatant form. Still, until all is accomplished and the other, unknown shore is reached the Law must remain lest human life become chaotic and brutal.

Those who have crossed over, to be sure, no longer need the Law, but only because they fulfill it in a deeper and more radical way than even the most fastidious Pharisees ever imagined. For those who live in this ego-constructed cosmos, the Law forbids murder. Those who have seen the illusory and corrupting nature of the ego and have faith into the light, however, know that all attacks [verbal or otherwise] upon another are to be avoided at all costs. To call a brother a fool is to attack both oneself and the light, for all men are one in him. It is like throwing rotten eggs at a movie screen because you do not like one of the actors.

In the ego world men are constantly concerned about their own honor and offenses against it. In the world of light losing face is of no importance. What is important is reconciliation with both fellow Israelite and enemy. The illumined one, without concern for his own pride, seeks out his alienated brother and accuser to effect unity. Only when that is accomplished does he express his at-one-ment with the Father through sacrifice.[7]

The old law also forbids adultery. Yeshua says, however, that the real problem is lust, the bondage of desire. The law against adultery exists to preserve the institution of marriage, one of the supporting pillars of human society. Yeshua, however, is not as concerned with the social fabric as with the age-old illusion of the self and its insecurities. The root problem which man faces is not the preservation of society but the persistent smoke screen which dims man's inner eye to the light. Open that eye, shake off man's perennial sense of insecurity, and lust will disappear.

Yeshua speaks of goudging out an eye or cutting off a hand if it offends, but he knows the problem lies much deeper than that. *If* it is the eye that offends, then the eye should be removed. In truth, however, it is not the eye itself but the old Adam, the ego, which must be amputated and destroyed. There must be a complete death and rebirth if the essential problem is to be solved. Needless to say, such a crucifixion is not easy, for the old ego is no mean adversary. He is the *diabolé* himself and uses every trick to confuse and corrupt. Still, Yeshua holds out the hope that the crossing can be made, that the cosmos can be rent, and that the light can and will shine forth.

The question remains, however, as to whether, after illumination has "occurred," marriage is still possible. Does the negation of erotic love mean the end of all positive sexual relations? Both Yeshua and Gautama Siddartha recognize erotic love to be a central problem in man's life which must be rooted out. Both also pointed to the ego as the cause of that love. Does this mean that marriage and sex are evils which the enlightened man must forego? Or can marriage and sex exist without lust? Is there such a thing as sexual desire without egotism?

It is usually assumed that Gautama took a negative view concerning sex while Yeshua, as a good Jew, took a much more positive one.[8] Surely, however, it is not that simple, particularly when one is dealing with Yeshua. One of the key passages which may shed light upon the brief remarks about lust, marriage, and divorce in the Sermon on the Mount is to be found in Matthew 19:3-12.

> And the Pharisees came up to him and tested him by asking, "Is it lawful to divorce one's wife for any cause? He answered, "Have you not read that he who made them from the beginning made them male and female and said, 'For this reason a man shall leave his father and mother and be joined to his wife, and the two shall become one? So they are no longer two but one. What therefore God has joined together, let no man put asunder."
>
> They said to him, "Why then did Moses command one to give a certificate of divorce, and to put away?" He said to them, "For your hardness of heart Moses allowed you to divorce your wives, but from the beginning it was not so. And I say to you whoever divorces his wife, except for unchastity, and marries another, commits adultery.
>
> The disciples said to him, "If such is the case of a man with his wife, it is not expedient to marry. But he said to them, "Not all men can receive this precept, but only those to whom it is given. For there are eunuchs

who have been so from birth, there are eunuchs who have been made eunuchs by men, and there are eunuchs who have made themselves eunuchs for the sake of the kingdom of heaven. He who is able to receive this, let him receive it."

Matt. 19:3-12

Clearly, Yeshua begins by expressing a very positive attitude toward marriage. Marriage is, in fact, the recreation of Adam, the reformation of his own body. As such, it represents a triumph over the ego of each individual.[9] In marriage the old egos are discarded as two come to live as one. Marriage is life now, together, without distinction. True marriage is the joyful fruit of illumination.

Divorce, then, is a sign that the kingdom has not come and that the wiley old ego still rules. Hence, Yeshua speaks in the most radical way against divorce. It is the ego breaking up the primal unity which God has joined together, a sign that illusion still takes precedence over light.

From the point of view of the ego, of course, Yeshua's words are extraordinarily demanding. It is easy to see why the disciples express their chagrin. Who would ever wish to enter into marriage if no divorce is possible? Could it not become a living hell? Would it not be better to abstain entirely?

Yeshua's response is tantalizingly enigmatic. He does emphasize that he is not setting forth a general law which all must accept. Only those "to whom it is granted" can enjoy marriage in this way. But what does he mean in his remarks about eunuchs? Does he really mean that for the sake of the kingdom some should literally castrate themselves? If so, Yeshua is even more negative about sex than Gautama.

Exegetes differ considerably about this matter and provide no general consensus for us at all.[10] Perhaps, however, Yeshua is teaching that marriage entered into for the sake of erotic lust and ego-building is no real marriage and ought to be avoided for the sake of the kingdom. Marriage founded upon the illusory claims and demands of the ego is not a genuine marriage and, therefore, instead of reflecting the kingdom of heaven leads men and women into the fires of Gehenna. Thus the Jewish tradition is correct in emphasizing the high value of marriage, but only if it is the sort of marriage which is described in Genesis as having taken place "once upon a time."

Parenthetically, though Yeshua seems to take a dim view of most so-called marriages that attitude in no way affects his feelings toward the offspring of those alliances. In Matthew the passage just cited is followed immediately by Yeshua's welcome to the children and his remark that "of such are the kingdom of heaven." For Yeshua every person is a child of the Father; one does not have to be an adult to enter the kingdom. In fact, because the child's ego-trail is shorter and less fixed, a child can, perhaps, cross over more easily. In any event, entering into the kingdom has nothing to do with the quality of the parent's marriage, with age, or with intellectual sophistication. In many respects, the less sophistication, the better.

After reinterpreting the law concerning marriage and divorce, Yeshua turns to the question of oaths and vows. Clearly he is, here, directing his attention to both the ninth "word" of the Decalogue and the ancient commandment, "You shall not take the name of the Lord your God in vain." As usual, he accepts these commandments but then extends their meaning, this time to include all oaths sworn with reference to heaven, earth, the holy city, or anything else.

At first glance, it would seem that Yeshua is now indulging in trivia, magnifying the importance of a person's words all out of proportion to their meaning. What is wrong in swearing "by heaven" or "by all that I hold sacred," etc. Why does Yeshua emphasize that such words come directly from the "evil one?" How is it that he mentions such a minor matter in so important a sermon?

In truth, however, the matter is not minor at all, though it may appear so from the vantage point of the ego. There are at least three reasons why an oath sworn by anything reveals that the old deluder is hard at work. First, such an oath assumes the great value or permanence of what is sworn by when in fact it is only a part of the ever-changing cosmic dance. Second, the oath implies control over the self's actions if not what is sworn by, when the ego, that dead past, can actually control nothing. And third, oaths imply that there are levels of truth and trustworthiness when in fact there ought to be only one level. If someone says "Yes" or "No", the addition of "by heaven" adds nothing but an indication that the speaker is trapped in the old illusions.

Of course, the forsaking of oaths does not dispel the illusions of the ego. Yeshua is not offering here any new law. All that he is saying is that the illumined man needs to say no more than "Yes" or "No." Heaping up empty phrases is of no value at all. In effect, however, Yeshua is undercutting one of the cornerstones of both religious and civil law. In the world distinctions are constantly being made between promises and iron-clad contracts, between statements and testimony made under oath, between sweet-no-things and marriage vows. Yeshua teaches that for the enlightened one there is no distinction; either words mean what they say or they do not. If the latter is the case, (which is implied when a special oath must be taken) the old ego is obviously at work.

Even more radical are Yeshua's teachings about the old nomadic law of retaliation, "An eye for an eye and a tooth for a tooth." Once the ego has been conquered and overcome such a reaction to those who attack becomes quite unnecessary and indeed unwarranted. To respond to the thief or the Roman soldier in a retaliatory way is simply an expression of the old man. Worldly goods bring no security. Therefore, if someone demands money or a coat or anything else from you, give it away freely. Set yourself free from erotic love which offers the illusory security of the evil one.

What sense, after all, does defending an illusory ego make? The illumined observer of the cosmic drama need not take sides; he is secure in the light; he is rooted in the Unknown. He is, in truth, nothing and hence is beyond attack. This does not mean that the true disciple is apathetic. The eros which motivates the old man is replaced by agape, that even-handed, transcendent love which pays no attention at all to the insecurities of the ego. Hence, the illumined man loves his friends and his enemies equally. His concern for man is like the sun which shines on the just and the unjust alike. His concern is not for self-justification and protection but that all men may see the light and forsake the powers of darkness.

Yeshua does not counsel just a little less egotism or a little more compassion. The movement of which he speaks cracks the cosmos wide open; it is the passage from death to life, from the old Adam to the New. One does not, in the last analysis, grow into the new condition slowly. One must pass through gates that open and close instantaneously. To move too slowly is to be sliced in half.

Ch'an Buddhists in China have spoken of *wu*, that nontemporal moment when the Great Divide is crossed and the inner eye is activated.[11] Yeshua intimates a similar movement when one passes from the realm of the old ego into the realm of perfection. Yeshua doesn't mean that each person must try his best to defeat the ego. That would be like trying to lift oneself by one's own bootstraps. When the ego triumphs over the ego, an even greater illusion is born. A presumably perfect ego is the most dangerous idol known to man.

No, perfection *is now*; the wholeness and completeness cannot be achieved because they already are. All that remains to be done is to dispel the mists of illusion—a task which the ego is admirably ill-suited to perform. But if not the ego, who then?

IV. Religion

> Beware of practicing your piety before men in order to be seen by them; for then you will have no reward from your Father who is in heaven.
>
> Thus, when you give alms, sound no trumpet before you, as the hypocrites do in the synagogues and in the streets, that they may be praised by men. Truly, I say to you, they have their reward. But when you give alms, do not let your left hand know what your right hand is doing, so that your alms may be in secret; and your Father who sees in secret will reward you.
>
> And when you pray, you must not be like the hypocrites; for they love to stand and pray in the synagogues and at the street corners, that they may be seen by men. Truly, I say to you, they have their reward. But when you pray, go into your room and shut the door and pray to your Father who is in secret; and your Father who sees in secret will reward you.
>
> Matt. 6:1-6

Religion, with its rites and rituals and discipline is usually considered the primary means by which individuals seek for and find enlightenment.[12] "Religion is the bond which binds God and man together." Yeshua does not totally deny this; as a good Jew he celebrates Tabernacles and Passover, observes the Law (albeit in his own fashion), and employs various religious symbols and concepts in his teaching. Nevertheless, he is also keenly aware that religion, far from always bringing enlightenment, may foster the worst form of ego-illusion. Significantly, his greatest foes are not the religious skeptics or the immoral outcasts but the leaders of the religious community: the scribes, Sadducees, and Pharisees.

In this compendium of his teachings it is interesting that his remarks about religious practice are largely, if not wholly, negative. Essentially, what he wishes to guard against is the use of religion as a prop for the ego, a function which it more often than not serves. To undercut this misuse of religion, Yeshua counsels secrecy. Do not, he says, let anyone see or know of your piety. If you give alms, do it in secret. Don't even tell yourself what you are doing for that will only make you more and more proud of your ego. If you pray, go and hide; *do not* pray in public. *Do not* let anyone else know that you pray. Only the Father should know what you are doing. And when you pray, use only the briefest petitions, as in the so-called Lord's Prayer.

A full analysis of this prayer is, of course, beyond the scope of our brief survey. Within the context of the Sermon of the Mount the main point of its inclusion here is as an example of brevity. Nevertheless, the prayer is so pregnant with meaning that we must linger over it for a few moments, if only to provide a new translation and running commentary.

Our Father in the heavens

Yeshua begins the prayer by addressing it to a figure familiar in world mythology, i.e., the Father God who lives in the heavens.[13] In so doing, he also implies a basic dichotomy—between heaven and earth—which is likewise known the world over. Whether or not we can believe in a spatialized God who lives "up there," the Father appears, within the context of the myth, in the heavens, for the landscape of the story is the landscape of man's mythic imagination.[14] In the realm where the myth is acted out, the unseen but not unheard Father sits above upon his throne while the Son performs his heroic acts on earth, thereby saving men from the fires of Gehenna which crackle beneath the feet.

> May your name be sanctified,
> May your kingdom come,
> May your will appear:
> As in the heavens, so on earth.

Any translation of these lines is bound to be somewhat clumsy, for English, unlike Greek has no third person imperative form. It is important, however, to preserve the parallelism so clearly evident in the Greek, for it expresses the unfolding of a basic idea: the dichotomy between heaven and earth, light and darkness, God and man must be overcome.

God's name, which was regarded by Jews as too holy to pronounce, is more than just a sacred verbal formula. It is the manifestation of the Father's reality among men. Yeshua teaches men to pray for the setting apart of this name, not by men, but by God himself. It is the Father who is called upon to sanctify the name, send the kingdom and reveal in action his will. These lines are an expression of the belief that if the dichotomy between light and darkness is to be overcome only the light can do the abolishing.

> Give us the bread we need,
> And cancel our debts as we cancel the debts
> of those who are indebted us,
> And do not bring us to the test, but draw
> us away from the evil one.

The first line of the text is difficult to translate adequately for the meaning of *epiousion* (usually rendered "daily") is uncertain. Here, for lack of evidence, it is translated "that we need." Although some translations render *opheilemata* as trespasses or sins, it clearly means "what is owed" or "debts" and has rather monetary connotations. As is so often the case, Yeshua brings his message down to a very common, harsh level of reality.[15] If you want your debts cancelled, you must first be willing to cancel the debts of others. If you want others to pay you, then you must expect to pay others. To be sure, Yeshua uses debts as an illustration and exemplification of the way in which man's relation to

God and his relation to men are intertwined. Still, the basically monetary focus of his teaching ought not to be blurred, for there are many who like to forgive in the abstract but still believe that "business is business."

Yeshua was, as we have already seen, driven into the wilderness to be tested by the *diabolé*. As the Father's chosen one he passed the test triumphantly, but the rest of us are not so likely to dispel the illusions of the ego as easily as he did. The final petition, therefore, calls upon the Father to draw us away from the evil one into the realm of light lest we fail the test and become entrapped once more in the web of illusion.

One of the noteworthy features of Yeshua's teaching is that although he preaches repentance and faith and calls men to illumination, he seems to teach no particular discipline through which men can reach that goal. Gautama Siddartha, according to some early accounts, adopted certain yogic practices from contemporary Indian religion and adapted them for the purposes of his followers.[16] Yeshua, however, says nothing about any meditational discipline apart from prayer. How then can he be called a teacher of enlightenment?

The problem for both Yeshua and Gautama is that meditational and other religious practices are employed by the ego and hence can be instruments for a new round of ego-building. Moreover, those who have crossed over repeatedly tell us that ultimately there is no method which will produce the illuminating breakthrough of which we speak. Faith "comes"; it cannot be manufactured.

Like Gautama, Yeshua commends to his disciples the usual religious practices of his culture: alms-giving, prayer, fasting— but with the added proviso of secrecy. This, in effect, is his central discipline. Whatever religious or meditational technique you use, use it in secret. Never tell anyone of your "experience." Try as best you can not to reveal to anyone that you are fasting. Anoint your head, wash your face, lest people discover what you are doing, admire you for it, and hence build up exactly what needs to be destroyed. The "reward" for (or better the response to) this secrecy from the Heavenly Father is not described, but surely it is precisely the opposite of the ego-supporting rewards most of us want.

The follower of Yeshua, then, should be only secretly pious. Outwardly, he may conform to "local custom" but does nothing cultic to inspire admiration or praise. Religious observance is *not* the way in which he lets his light shine before men. One wonders, then, in what sense Yeshua's message is really religious at all. Surely it is difficult to understand how a worldwide religion could be founded upon the basis of such absolute, personal secrecy. Nevertheless, this is his clear teaching. Is the visible, institutional Church, then, no more than an outward, cultural husk—a part of the cosmic dance—which has only tangential relation to Yeshua's teaching?

V. The Keys of the Kingdom

The final section of the Sermon on the Mount is composed of a variety of sayings which seem at first to be only loosely woven together. Despite this apparent lack of systematic order of these twelve sayings, they form an excellent summary of Yeshua's teaching and stand, as it were, as the keys of the kingdom.

> 1. Do not lay up for yourselves treasures on earth, where moth and rust consume and where thieves break in and steal, but lay up for yourselves treasures in heaven, where neither moth nor rust consumes and where thieves do not break in and steal. For where your treasure is, there will your heart be also.
>
> Matt. 6:19-21

Predictably, Yeshua begins this portion of the sermon by attacking the idea that security is to be found in the goods of this world. He commends instead finding one's treasure and security in that realm of light, designated mythically here as heaven.

Since we have already dealt with this subject at some length there is no need to add further elaboration except to underline again for our affluent age Yeshua's supreme distrust of laying up earthly treasures. In a word, he cuts at the very root of our modern, capitalistic society. Not that he provides for us an alternative system. Indeed all systems of this world express inevitably man's eros. Rather Yeshua counsels us to step out of the system and to find our meaning elsewhere.

2. The eye is the lamp of the body. So, if your eye is
    sound, your whole body will be full of light; but if
    your eye is not sound, your whole body will be full
    of darkness. If then the light in you is darkness,
    how great is the darkness!

    Matt. 6:22-23

How does one lay up treasure in heaven? By opening the inner,
wisdom eye to the light of illumination.[17] The problem, however,
is that like the recipient of Yeshua's curing power in John 9, men
are born blind. The inner eye is there but is diseased. Most people
may receive flickerings of that celestial radiance which plays
about us—but only flickerings. The illumined alone see clearly.

Yeshua's mission is to heal that inner eye and to open it to the
light. When the cure is effected, it is not that man can see God as
an object but that the whole body is filled with light. The illumination is not perceived but is that by which a glorious new form of
perception can occur.

3. No one can serve two masters; for either he will
    hate the one and love the other, or he will be de-
    voted to the one and despise the other. You cannot
    serve God and mammon.

    Matt. 6:24

Once the eye has been opened a radical divide is crossed. There
is no possibility of living in the two worlds at once. Either one
identifies oneself with one's ego and searches for security
through "mammon" or one finds security in the divine light
alone and floats with faith. To think that one can open the eye to
the light and continue the old task of ego-propping is itself
illusory.

4. Therefore I tell you, do not be anxious about your
    life, what you shall eat or what you shall drink, nor
    about your body, what you shall put on. Is not life
    more than food, and the body more than clothing?
    Look at the birds of the air: they neither reap nor
    gather into barns, and yet your heavenly Father
    feeds them. Are you not of more value than they?
    And which of you by being anxious can add one
    cubit to his span of life? And why are you anxious
    about clothing? Consider the lilies of the field, how

they grow; they neither toil nor spin; yet I tell you, even Solomon in all his glory was not arrayed like one of these. But if God so clothes the grass of the field, which today is alive and tomorrow is thrown into the oven, will he not much more clothe you, O men of little faith? Therefore do not be anxious, saying, "What shall we eat?" or "What shall we drink?" or "What shall we wear?" For the Gentiles seek all these things; and your heavenly Father knows that you need them all. But seek first his kingdom and his righteousness, and all these things shall be yours as well.

Therefore do not be anxious about tomorrow, for tomorrow will be anxious for itself. Let the day's own trouble be sufficient for the day.

Matt. 6:25-34

What is life like on the other side of the instantaneously closing doors, in the realm of faith? What is man's life when filled with light to be? Essentially it is a life which no longer takes seriously the ego or the world's threats upon it. It is living now, in the present, without anxiety. He who has crossed over does not worry about food or clothing or anything else. Like the lilies of the field and the birds of the air he depends wholly upon the divine light for sustenance.[18]

The enlightened one lives an extraordinarily simple, yet amazingly rich life. He does not live for tomorrow but concentrates wholly upon today. For him the lily shimmers with a beauty the old Masters only groped for but never captured. He wants little and enjoys much. He does not aim to make a name for himself and yet excels at what he does. Like the birds of the air he wings his way gracefully through life.

But, one is bound to say, isn't this a wholly impractical and unworkable way of life? From the vantage point of the ego and its illusions it surely is. No one who believes in good American common sense could conceivably accept this. It goes against the grain of everything we know and believe. But then, Yeshua doesn't pretend to be teaching American common sense. He does not maintain that he is providing a workable ethic for the world. He is describing the life of those who have repented and crossed over. He is dispelling illusions.

6. Judge not, that you be not judged. For with the judgment you pronounce you will be judged, and the measure you give will be the measure you get. Why do you see the speck that is in your brother's eye, but do not notice the log that is in your own eye? Or how can you say to your brother, "Let me take the speck out of your eye," when there is the log in uour own eye? You hypocrite, first take the log out of your own eye, and then you will see clearly to take the speck out of your brother's eye.

Matt 7:1-5

The illumined life is a life of non-discrimination. No longer does one say, "This is good and that is bad," for one is beyond pleasure and pain, reward and threat. He who has crossed over loves all men indiscriminately, without regard to intent or action. Thieves and murderers stand with bishops and kings in the cast of characters which acts out the drama before us. Why should one love the one more than the other? Are they not all united in that one light?

From the vantage point of those who have crossed over all human judging is both ludicrous and tragic. It is ludicrous because it is invariably but an example of one blind man attacking another because the latter cannot see. The whole human comedy is one of delusion and ignorance in which the actors flail about in the darkness.

At the same time, it is tragic because every ego-action has its deleterious effects. The more one judges, the more one is entangled in the illusion of good and evil, the more the ego feels threatened by judgement. Every sneer at another is a sneer at oneself, for ultimately all men are one. Like the Indian doctrine of *karma*, Yeshua's teachings emphasize that built into the cosmos is a law of just retribution.[19] The judgment you give is the judgment you get. Each ego constitutes its own hell.

Paradoxically, it is precisely the person who understands the lunacy of judging because his inner eye has been opened to the light who is in the best position to judge. He now understands that to which others are blind and can effectively remove specks which are impediments to clear sight. Judgment is for him, however, a healing art, not a form of ego-protection. Yeshua offers words of condemnation, but not to justify himself. The sword which he wields is a healing sword, for it cuts through the bonds of egotism and desire. Like any good surgeon, he removes the deleterious, offending malignancy, not to destroy but to cure.

The unenlightened man judges others in order to justify what he thinks to be himself and in so doing expresses eros. The enlightened man judges others in order to heal them and in so doing expresses undiscriminating agape. One of the great dangers of life is to pretend to do the latter when, in fact, one is doing the former. That was the fault of the religious leaders at the time of Yeshua and it was for that reason that his words of warning to them are invariably so harsh.

> 7. Do not give dogs what is holy; and do not throw your pearls before swine, lest they trample them under foot and turn to attack you.
>
> Matt. 7:6

Although the turning from darkness to light is finally sudden and cataclysmic, there are degrees of blindness among men. To speak of the life beyond to someone who has not even seen the least glimmering of celestial light with his inner eye is like throwing precious stones to swine. They will be angry because they expected swill and find the jewels quite indigestible. Chances are they will only grind the stones into the mud and blame the feeder for the lack of proper food.

In the case of men, intolerance and reprisal are predictable responses because the light appears as a dire threat to those who spend their time protecting their egos. What could be more offensive than considering oneself an illusion which must be dispelled? What could be more disruptive than the suggestion that one should give away everything for the sake of nothing? The enlightened one must take care lest his words be turned to foolishness by the worldly wise and clever.

> 8. Ask, and it will be given you; seek, and you will find; knock, and it will be opened to you. For everyone who asks receives, and he who seeks finds, and to him who knocks it will be opened. Or what man of you, if his son asks him for bread, will give him a stone? Or if he asks for a fish, will give him a serpent? If you then, who are evil, know how to give good gifts to your children, how much more

will your Father who is in heaven give good things
to those who ask him!

Matt. 7:7-11

The ordinary man, wrapped as he is in darkness, finds little
correlation between what he prays for and what he receives. He
wants, above all, security for himself; yet this is exactly what is
denied him. When this denial comes clear, prayer in his mouth
becomes an expression of either desperation or religious cyni-
cism. When he hears these words of Yeshua his response is either
sheer disbelief or amazement. How could Yeshua make such a
ludicrous claim as this?

Yeshua, however, speaks not of the old man whose petitions
are invariably ego-oriented but of him who has passed over, of
the new Adam. The illumined one whose inner eye has been
opened lives in unity with the light; his body is filled with light.
Hence, there is no discrepancy between wish and fulfillment,
between prayer and response to prayer. The Enlightened One
wills the divine will.

This does not mean, however, that the new man is but a
passive and obedient instrument. Yeshua teaches no doctrine of
kismet.[20] On the contrary, he teaches repeatedly that the enlightened one will have the use of extraordinary powers, powers
which he, himself, exhibits in his own ministry.

Although his claims may surprise us, there is nothing particularly unusual about them. In many parts of the world, men who
have gained enlightenment have attested to the phenomenal
powers which such crossing over can bring. Clairvoyance, the
remembrance of events from other lives, control over physical
phenomena (even the power to resurrect from the grave) have
been claimed by various Indian, Chinese, and Tibetan holy
men.[21] Yeshua himself reveals many of these powers when he
walks on water, predicts the future, tells others what they are
thinking, raises Lazarus from the grave, etc. Nor does he restrict
such powers to himself. On the contrary, he indicates that true
faith brings with it a control over the illusory cosmos which most
people would deem impossible. In one memorable passage he
says.

> If you had faith as a grain of mustard seed, you could
> say to this sycamine tree, "Be rooted up, and be
> planted in the sea," and it would obey you.
>
> Luke 17:6

Because these words have always seemed difficult to accept,
the Church has devoted considerable time and effort to their
reinterpretation. Nevertheless, the plain sense of the words remains; Yeshua states rather clearly that true faith entails the
development of what we might call magical power.[22] An equally
clear example of this is to be found in at least some very early
versions of the Gospel of Mark. The last chapter of that Gospel
shows the risen Christ describing to his disciples what the signs
associated with believers are:

> In my name they will cast out devils; they will have the
> gift of tongues; they will pick up snakes in their hands,
> and be unharmed should they drink deadly poison;
> they will lay their hands on the sick, who will recover.
>
> Mark 16:17-18

Many a liberal theologian heaved a great sigh of relief when
early manuscripts showed that this passage may not have been
"original."[23] From our point of view that fact makes little difference. One could argue conversely that early Christians were so
sure that faith entailed miracles that they dared to add this passage to the received text in order to make that point clear. At the
very least we can say that early Christianity made claims comparable to those made by other world religions. Illumination not
only removes the illusions of the cosmos but actually gives the
man of faith some control over it. If the cosmos is like a projected
film and the illumined one is at one with the projected light, what
things are not possible?

> So whatever you wish that men would do to you, do
> so to them, for this is the law and the prophets.
>
> Matt. 7:12

After such literally earth-shattering thoughts Yeshua brings us
quickly back to a topic more akin to our own common sense. The
enlightened one may develop phenomenal powers but they are
always to be tempered by that touchstone of human morality, the

golden rule. Needless to say, however, this rule, when taken out of context and placed in the hands of the ego, can be a dangerous guide indeed. The ego loves flattery, affluence, and power. Is this then what should be bestowed upon others? To take the ego's desires as normative is to found a mutual admiration society but hardly to express *agape*.

No, Yeshua means this guideline also for the one whose ego has been overcome. His disciples are not encouraged to prop up the egos of others but to treat all men as one in the light. In other words, in order to know clearly what "you would have them do unto you," one must pass through the needle's eye to freedom. At the same time, this basic guideline provides a suitable corrective for the abuse of kingdom power. The illumined may develop potencies quite unknown to the common person but he must always use them to express, not his own desires but his compassion for other persons.

9. Enter by the narrow gate; for the gate is wide and the way is easy that leads to destruction, and those who enter by it are many. For the gate is narrow and the way is hard, that leads to life, and those who find it are few.

Matt. 7:13-14

Usually, the founder of a great world religion is taken as providing a message which is meant for all men. Otherwise, it would not be a world religion. In one sense, Yeshua does this; his teaching is thoroughly universal. As Paul was to observe later, in Christ there is neither Jew nor Greek, there is neither slave nor free, there is neither male nor female. (Galatians 3:28) Nevertheless, Yeshua is equally aware of how few will ever really follow him. Never in his mind does he seem to envision a vast movement in which the world is converted to Christianity.

There are two ways: the way of the ego and the way of light. Most men will not even begin to shake themselves loose from the delusions of the ego. Only the few will find that narrow defile which leads through the impassable mountains to the Promised Land. Yeshua knows full well that his gospel is not one which will sweep society. To make his teachings the cornerstone for a public institution meant for everyone is one of the sillier crimes ever perpetrated in the name of God. Even the disciples who have followed Yeshua thus far are cautioned that his way is supremely difficult and that they must not take it for granted. To think that the ego-ridden man, with only glimmerings of the celestial radiance will readily follow Yeshua's teachings is to misconstrue the whole of the gospel.

> 10. Beware false prophets, who come to you in sheep's clothing but inwardly are ravenous wolves. You will know them by their fruits. Are grapes gathered from thorns, or figs from thistles? So, every sound tree bears good fruit, but the bad tree bears evil fruit. A sound tree cannot bear evil fruit, nor can a bad tree bear good fruit. Every tree that does not bear good fruit is cut down and thrown into the fire. Thus you will know them by their fruits.
>
> Matt. 7:15-20

Yeshua is well aware how easily his message can be corrupted. He knows about those religious egotists who pretend humility but really find religious leadership a great support for their self-images. That may very well be what most religions are all about: people play-acting with faith, people mouthing religious sentiments to increase their own ego-power.

All that Yeshua can do at this point is to warn his disciples that such prophets will come and lead men astray if great care is not taken. "Do not just listen to their works," he says; "Observe their deeds." Have these prophets of religion genuinely given up all desire for affluence, influence, and power? Is their love truly indiscriminate? Do they live like the lilies of the field and birds of the air? Are they genuinely secretive about their religious lives?

If the answer to these questions is "no," then beware them. Their fruits show that they have not been illumined and have not passed over. At best they are but blind men leading the blind. At worst, they are wolves in sheep's clothing, consciously looking for their own gain.

> 11. Not every one who says to me, "Lord, Lord," shall enter the kingdom of heaven, but he who does the will of my Father who is in heaven. On that day many will say to me, "Lord, Lord did we not

> prophesy in your name, and cast out demons in
> your name, and do many mighty works in your
> name?" And then will I declare to them, "I never
> knew you; depart from me, you evildoers."
>
> Matt. 7:21-23

What matters most is not theology or doctrine or even great works but illumination and passing over. Unless a man has passed through death to life, no calling on the name of Yeshua matters. There are all sorts of people who claim to follow him, who prophesy, cure, even do miracles in his name who are still thoroughly trapped in the illusions against which Yeshua fights. Many believe themselves to be his true disciples. But are they? Has the light really shone? Yeshua will say to them, "Away from me you evil men."

> 12. Everyone then who hears these words of mine
> and does them will be like a wise man who built
> his house upon the rock; and the rain fell, and the
> floods came, and the winds blew and beat upon
> that house, but it did not fall, because it had been
> founded on the rock. And everyone who hears
> these words of mine and does not do them will be
> like a foolish man who built his house upon the
> sand; and the rain fell, and the floods came, and
> the winds blew and beat against the house, and it
> fell; and great was the fall of it.
>
> Matt. 7:24-27

The only firm support in life is the light of the world. All other props and stays slip quickly into the sand or are washed away with the flood. It is like a small child pretending to swim while keeping one hand on the sandy bottom. When the undertow comes, he shall be swept away and drowned.

Many Christians have read these words, but how few have believed them! How many of the great Church leaders and thinkers have relaxed their grip and let go of their little supports? How many theologians have seriously considered trying what he suggests? Is not their answer almost invariably that what Yeshua has suggested is impossible; therefore, we will substitute our own best wisdom for his. But if true illumination is impossible then let us forget it and return to the land where egos dwell. Let us forget Yeshua and his call for crucifixion of the self as itself delusion. Surely one cannot have it both ways; the name of Yeshua but not his Way!

> And when Jesus finished these sayings, the crowds were astonished at his teachings, for he taught them as one who had authority, and not as their scribes.
>
> Matt. 7:28-29

No major modern translation quite catches the power of this sentence, for neither "were astonished" (R.S.V.) nor "were astounded" (N.E.B.) nor "were deeply impressed" (Anchor Bible), nor "made a deep impression upon" (Jerusalem) expresses fully the power of the verb *ekplosso*. Better might be "were driven into a panic" or "were driven away," for Yeshua's message is more than simply surprising or impressive. From beginning to end Yeshua turns the world upside down, undercutting our most precious common sense, calling into question our most sacred values.

What panics the crowd, however, are not his theories or radical ideas. In fact, nothing which Yeshua teaches is the least bit theoretical or speculative. He offers no new cosmology or theological formula or ethic. Neither does he set forth a new rendering of the ancient Hebrew or some variant reading of the text. What astounds, shocks, and panics his hearers is rather his *exousia*—what the English translation calls "authority." What is meant is not that Yeshua speaks gravely or cogently or even assuredly. The scribes speak like that. Rather, what makes Yeshua's teaching unique is his power to do what he says. He is his message. He speaks, not as someone working out some new ideas but as someone in touch with the basic energy which animates and illumines the cosmos. The crowds sense this and are driven down the mountain in absolute panic, like sinners fleeing the wrath of God. What Yeshua brought as a boon becomes, it would appear, a terrifying blight. The good news is heard as words of woe.

5

THE DISCIPLES AND THE CHRIST

I. The Disciples

And he called to him his twelve disciples and gave them authority over unclean spirits, to cast them out, and to heal every disease and every infirmity. The names of the twelve apostles are these: first, Simon, who is called Peter, and Andrew his brother; James the son of Zebedee, and John his brother; Philip and Bartholomew; Thomas and Matthew the tax collector; James the son of Alphaeus, and Thaddeus; Simon the Cananaean, and Judas Iscariot, who betrayed him.

These twelve Jesus sent out, charging them, "Go nowhere among the Gentiles, and enter no town of the Samaritans, but go rather to the lost sheep of the house of Israel. And preach as you go, saying, "The kingdom of heaven is at hand." Heal the sick, raise the dead, cleanse lepers, cast out demons. You received without pay; give without pay. Take no gold, nor silver, nor copper in your belts, no bag for your journey, nor two tunics, nor sandals, nor a staff; for the laborer deserves his food. And whatever town or village you enter, find out who is worthy in it, and stay with him until you depart. As you enter the house, salute it. And if the house is worthy, let your peace return to you. And if any one will not receive you or listen to your words, shake off the dust from your feet as you leave that house or town. Truly, I say to you, it shall be more tolerable on the day of judgment for the

75

land of Sodom and Gomorrah than for that town.

Matt. 10:1-15

T he crowd, like the ocean tide, recedes in panic before the overwhelming power of Yeshua only to flow back to him once more, attracted by that same *exousia* (authority) which had driven them away. In response to their exigencies, he heals the sick of their diseases, casts out demons, and even raises one of the departed from the dead. Yeshua seems to want no publicity (Matthew 9:30) but there is no way to keep such matters quiet. Soon the news of his miraculous actions spreads across the land. Kingdom power is manifest everywhere, even among the Gentiles.

At the same time, Yeshua seems to become more and more reluctant to speak plainly to the people, resorting to parables which those not "in the know" find cryptic and confusing. Only to his disciples does he explain the meaning of these parables and express in a more straightforward way his own teaching. By and large, however, the Gospels contain the words which Yeshua directs to the crowds; only occasionally are there hints of his more secret teachings.

The Church, for the most part, has rejected the idea that Yeshua had an esoteric message which is not expressed in the Bible, and for good reason. Since that secret teaching was apparently lost at an early time, it was very easy for various charlatans to supplant his secret ideas with notions of their own. This seems to have been what the whole Gnostic dispute was about.[1] Nevertheless, it appears clear that Yeshua did train his disciples for their mission in ways at which we can only guess. Suddenly Peter and his compatriots reappear in view, filled with a power (*exousia*) which can be used to heal and perform other miracles. So transformed are they that when they are called up before authorities, they can speak through and with the Spirit of the Father.[2] In other words, they have become both wonder workers and prophets of the light.

These facts alone would indicate that Yeshua's teaching to his inner circle was not primarily of a doctrinal or intellectual type. What he effects in the disciples is not so much a change in ideas as a transformation which leads to empowerment. The light is not a theory to be expounded but that by which one sees and acts.

Yeshua as a teacher is certainly closer to Gautama than to Aristotle. He is not interested in cosmology or theology or ethics. What he teaches is transformation through enlightenment.

Around Yeshua cluster twelve disciples (*Matheteke*), like the twelve tribes of Israel around Jacob or, perhaps, like the twelve moons (months) around the sun.[4] Each so reflects the light of the One in the center that he, too, can heal, cast out demons, and cause Satan to fall from the heights. Yeshua has communicated this power for no pay—he is no Sophist or professional academician—therefore his disciples are to dispense it freely.[5]

Whether this power is something inherent in man which Yeshua unleases or is bestowed upon the disciples from without is not made clear. What is evident (Matt. 10:25) is that gradually, as their power and wisdom increase they will become like Yeshua and take on disciples too.[6] Thus the movement spreads.

Unfortunately, this master-pupil relationship, so important in the Gospels, was apparently abandoned by the Church at a fairly early date and replaced by the preacher-listener pattern. The line of apostolic succession, according to tradition, was maintained and the rite of the laying on of hands, preserved, but the transmission of power gradually declined. The notion of the apostolic succession became primarily a way of defending doctrinal orthodoxy; the secrets of the kingdom: ego-loss and the concomitant blossoming of power, vanished; faith became its antithesis, i.e., submissive belief in the doctrines of the Church.

Yeshua sends out his inner circle with the sure conviction that they will find supporters on the way. They carry no money, no extra clothing, no staff, but depend wholly upon the hospitality of the "worthy." In response to the needed food and lodging, the disciples bestow their "Peace" upon the house. Doubtless this Peace was a much more powerful reality to them than a blessing would be to us. The disciples are full of holy power and in their Peace they communicate something of this power to the deserving. It would seem that this communication is, in fact, another result of Yeshua's instructions.[7] Unfortunately, however, neither the precise nature of this power nor how its communication can be achieved is any longer known. Like so many other secret teachings, it has been lost to both the Church and the world.

Behold, I send you out as sheep in the midst of wolves; so be wise as serpents and innocent as doves. Beware of men; for they will deliver you up to councils, and flog you in their synagogues, and you will be dragged before governors and kings for my sake, to bear testimony before them and the Gentiles. When they deliver you up, do not be anxious how you are to speak or what you are to say; for what you are to say will be given to you in that hour; for it is not you who speak, but the Spirit of your Father speaking through you. Brother will deliver up brother to death, and the father his child, and children will rise against parents and have them put to death; and you will be hated by all for my name's sake. But he who endures to the end will be saved. When they persecute you in one town, flee to the next; for truly, I say to you, you will not have gone through all the towns of Israel, before the Son of man comes.

A disciple is not above his teacher, nor a servant above his master; it is enough for the disciple to be like his teacher, and the servant like his master. If they have called the master of house Beelzebul, how much more will they malign those of his household.

So have no fear of them; for nothing is covered that will not be revealed, or hidden that will not be known. What I tell you in the dark, utter in the light; and what you hear whispered, proclaim upon the housetops. And do not fear those who kill the body but cannot kill the soul; rather fear him who can destroy both soul and body in hell. Are not two sparrows sold for a penny? And not one of them will fall to the ground without your Father's will. But even the hairs of your head are all numbered. Fear not, therefore; you are of more value than many sparrows. So every one who acknowledges me before man, I also will acknowledge before my Father who is in heaven; but whoever denies me before men, I also will deny before my Father who is in heaven.

Do not think that I have come to bring peace on earth; I have not come to bring peace, but a sword. For I have come to set a man against his father, and a daughter against her mother, and a daughter-in-law against her mother-in-law; and a man's foes will be those of his own household. He who loves father or mother more than me is not worthy of me; and he who loves son or daughter more than me is not worthy of me; and he who does not take his cross and follow me is not worthy of me. He who finds his life will lose it, but he who loses his life for my sake will find it.

He who receives you receives me, and he who receives me receives him who sent me. He who receives a prophet because he is a prophet shall receive a prophet's reward. And whoever gives to one of these little ones even a cup of cold water because he is a disciple, truly, I say to you, he shall not lose his reward." And when Jesus had finished instructing his twelve disciples, he went on from there to teach and preach in their cities.

Matt. 10:16-41

Although Yeshua knows that hospitable Jews will care for the disciples whom he sends out, he also knows the nasty and threatening way the light will be greeted in the world by others. There will be towns and villages where no warm welcome is offered at all. Officials in synagogues will not only be distrustful but may take harsh action. Disciples will find themselves in trouble with secular officials too and may, on account of the collaboration of Jew and Gentile, face death.

All this is quite understandable, for the light appears to the ego-world as an earth-shaking catastrophe. Few civil officials, religious leaders, or even ordinary men and women can accept it gladly, for the *exousia* of Yeshua undercuts the whole realm of ego support which most are anxious to preserve. Those who do respond positively, therefore, will immediately find themselves at odds with society, even with members of their own family. Indeed, it is exactly the family, that great source of human security which strongly resists the gospel. The man of faith severs these cords of erotic desire—especially evident in family life—which bind him to the world. Since mother and father are a part of cosmic illusion, they too must be forsaken for the light. Hence Yeshua says elsewhere,

If any one comes to me and does not hate his own
father and mother and wife and children and brothers
and sisters, yes, and even his own life, he cannot be
my disciple

Luke 16:26

Few can accept such strong medicine, for the hating of family
members seems much too harsh a reaction. We want to turn back,
if only for a moment, to say goodbye to our brothers or to bury
our dead father.[8] Yeshua, however, knows the dangers involved
in this temptation. The whole world of the ego is dead and must
be foregone if freedom is to be found. "Let the dead bury their
dead," he says. He who turns back is lost.

This sense of the ephemeral and illusory nature of the world
gives the man of faith fearlessness and power. He can stand
against Sanhedrin and king, knowing that they can, at most, kill
his already dead and illusory body. No man can destroy or even
harm the light of the world, for the light is no thing; it cannot be
attacked. Therefore, in the face of death the psyche of the illumined one remains undisturbed.

Consider for a moment, says Yeshua, those sparrows which
once chirped merrily in the trees but which now hang dead upon
a hook. That is what life in this cosmos is all about. Both life and
death are aspects of the same drama projected by the Father.
Death is no more threatening than life, for in it the light still
shines. There is only one enemy to fear: the enemy who can bring
both body and soul into Gehenna, the fiery garbage heap.[9] And
that enemy is the ego. He who has crossed over acts for the light,
radiates the light, and knows no fear. Only when the ego tempts
him to deny the light is he in mortal danger.

Yeshua knows, of course, that not everyone will fully recognize the light which he sends out and is quite willing to accept
various levels of recognition. Those who see in the disciples
prophets will be treated as prophets. Those who see holy men
will be treated as holy men. Even if the disciples are treated as
ordinary people in need there will be a reward. In other words,
the sort of acceptance provided actually says more about the
person doing the accepting than it does about the emissaries
themselves. The same situation still pertains today. The Gospels

are like a mirror: If a monkey looks in, there is little chance that he will see an apostle looking out.[10]

II. The Christ

> Now when Jesus came into the district of Caesarea Philippi, he asked his disciples, "Who do men say that the Son of Man is? And they said, "Some say John the Baptist, others say Elijah, and others Jeremiah or one of the prophets." He said to them, "But who do you say that I am?" Simon Peter replied, "You are the Christ, the Son of the living God." And Jesus answered him, "Blessed are you, Simon Bar-Jona! For flesh and blood has not revealed this to you, but my Father who is in heaven. And I tell you, you are Peter, and on this rock I will build my church, and the powers of death shall not prevail against it. I will give you the keys of the kingdom of heaven, and whatever you bind on earth shall be bound in heaven, and whatever you loose on earth shall be loosed in heaven." Then he strictly charged the disciples to tell no one that he was the Christ.
>
> Matt. 16:13-20

In both his teaching and his actions the hero must take care lest, in saying too much or acting too obviously he provide not the boon of freedom and security but the tyranny of dogmatism. Yeshua imparts to his disciples many secrets of the kingdom and empowers them with *exousia*, but of himself he says little.[11] As a mirror of the light he can only be and let his disciples see for themselves. Otherwise, there would be no true unveiling or breaking of the see. Thus does Yeshua speak parabolically and ambigously, employing the thought-forms and symbols of his own people in new and radically altered ways.

To him who does not see, for whom the eye has not been opened, the hero's teachings appear strange and bewildering. One hears them over and over again, marvelling at their strange inconsistency, searching for that key which will make sense out of the whole. The hero speaks with authority; he is not an ordinary pedagogue or preacher. We recognize the power that is here. Until the eye is opened, however, Yeshua, like all heroes, remains shrouded in darkness.

About half way through his brief career, such a moment of revelation occurs. Yeshua and his disciples have journeyed to the slopes of Mt. Hermon, to an area called Caesarea Philippi.[12] Here, in retreat from the crowds, Yeshua questions his disciples about his own impact upon the world. Who do people think he is? A number of answers connecting Yeshua with the long tradition of Hebrew prophets are given. When he asks his disciples for their opinion, however, Simon speaks up:

> You are the Christ, the Son of the living God.

Now, for the first time in the Synoptic Gospels, Yeshua is given by a man the title by which he has ever after been known.[13]

The term Christ (Christos) is, of course, simply a translation of the Hebrew word, Messiah, the anointed one. This term, in turn, is best understood when the ancient Israelite practice of king-making is comprehended. The ascension of a king to office in Israel took place in two stages: First, the king was anointed with oil, usually by a prophet, as a symbol of his election. Second, there followed the enthronment ceremonies themselves in which the king actually sat upon the throne and in so doing assumed the reins of office. Usually these two events were separated by only a short interval of time, but there were instances when a man was anointed but had to wait for several years before the enthrone-ment took place. David , for instance, was *Messiah* (anointed) long before he became *Melek* (king).[14]

After the destruction of the Israelite nation, the kingship itself fell into oblivion but the notion of a chosen one as the hope for Israel continued. The idea of the Messiah sometimes was laden with all sorts of ideas expressing Israel's hope for the future. Nevertheless, the notion of the Messiah as primarily a political hope was never wholly lost. In fact when Simon named Yeshua Christos, he may well have had in mind the image of an elected, soon-to-be-enthroned king. If so, Yeshua is identified as the hope of Israel in the sense that he is understood as a king who will eventually drive out the Gentile rulers, restore order, and estab-lish the throne of David once more. The added phrase "Son of God" underlines this belief, for it too was used as a title for the king in Israel's earlier years.[15] Clearly, however, if this is what

Simon means he is endowed with only a very limited understanding of what Yeshua has taught and is.

It is noteworthy that Yeshua highly commends Simon for what he has seen and, in fact, changes his name to Petros (Rock) because of this revelation to him. And because Petros has seen the kingly in him, Yeshua, in turn, makes Petros king, granting him keys to the kingdom of heaven. Like one with royal power, Petros' word is law. Whatever he binds is bound; whatever he looses is loosed. Thus he curiously becomes what he believes Yeshua to be.

Petros identifies Yeshua with a title which is to adhere to him throughout the ages. He is ever after called the Christ. The Christ which Yeshua is, however, bears only the most tangential relationship to the old conception of the Messiah—as Peter is soon to learn. No matter, Peter's identification of his teacher as more than a Rabbi or even a Prophet is seen to be God-given. *Christos* is accepted by Yeshua as a title and then is radically modified by him. This is a process which occurs repeatedly throughout the Gospels. Yeshua starts with the language and thought-forms of his culture; the husk of symbol is preserved, but the kernel of substance is thoroughly transformed.

From that time Jesus began to show his disciples that he must go to Jerusalem and suffer many things from the elders and chief priests and scribes, and be killed, and on the third day be raised. And Peter took him and began to rebuke him, saying, "God forbid, Lord! This shall never happen to you." But he turned and said to Peter, "Get behind me, Satan! You are a hindrance to me; for you are not on the side of God, but of men." Then Jesus told his disciples, "If any man would come after me, let him deny himself and take up his cross and follow me. For whosoever would save his life will lose it, and whoever loses his life for my sake will find it. For what will it profit a man, if he gains the whole world and forfeits his life? Or what shall a man give in return for his life? For the Son of man is to come with his angels in the glory of his Father, and then he will repay every man for what he has done. Truly, I say to you, there are some standing here who will not taste death before they see the Son of man coming in his kingdom.

Matt. 16:21-28

Immediately, Yeshua turns the idea of the Messiah upside down by making clear that he will go to Jerusalem, not to start a revolution whereby he will reestablish the throne of David, but to suffer and be killed. Peter's remonstrance shows how little he understands. Indeed, it would appear that none of Yeshua's hearers has gotten the point. The enemy is neither Herod Antipas nor the Roman officials nor even the religious establishment. The enemy is the ego.

Peter now sees in the mirror which is Yeshua an ego which is going to perish and hence protests. In response, Yeshua calls the man just invested as a king, Satan. And so he is. Man is only what he sees in the mirror. As soon as Peter sees the ego in his Master, he becomes, himself, the deluder. The hero will triumph only when he is rid of that illusion in fact as well as in theory. Disciples who do not understand this are working for the devil and are still trapped in the illusions of the old man. Indeed, a disciple who follows the master must not only recognize the enemy but must act similarly to defeat him. Crucifixion, the sluffing off of the old Adam, is the way, the only way, to salvation.

Moreover, Yeshua proclaims this to be a possibility for his disciples now. His message is no utopian dream which might come true in some far, far better world.

> There are some of these standing here who will not taste death before they see the Son of Man coming with his kingdom.

The inner eye is not closed forever. It can and will open and that landscape of divine light will become visible. It is true that such a prediction sounds like an apocalyptic promise about the imminence of the end of the world similar to those found in many contemporary Jewish writings. If it were actually meant to be only that, however, we should close the New Testament and turn to other matters. The end of the world, in the common sense meaning of that phrase, did not occur in that generation and Yeshua, therefore, was entirely wrong. And if he was wrong in

his apocalyptic visions how can we trust him about anything else?[16]
landscape becomes visible. The Son of Man, the glory of the
The fact is, however, that just as Yeshua radically reinterprets the conception of the Messiah so too does he fill the apocalyptic imagery with new meaning. As the eye of wisdom opens, the smoke screen called the cosmos dissolves; it is rolled up like an old carpet and burned in the fire. In its place that other luminous landscape becomes visible. The Son of Man, the glory of the Unknown, arrives with overwhelming brilliance.

This end of the world is not merely a psychological event as distinguished from a really physical one, for the cosmos itself is psychological. There is, ultimately, no distinction between the psychological and the physical. When enlightenment is accomplished, the Son of Man truly arrives and the world really comes to an end.

> And after six days Jesus took with him Peter and James and John his brother, and led them up a high mountain apart. And he was transfigured before them and his face shone like the sun, and his garments became white as light. And behold, there appeared to them Moses and Elijah, talking with him. And Peter said to Jesus, "Lord, it is well that we are here; if you wish, I will make three booths here, one for you and one for Moses and one for Elijah." He was still speaking, when lo, a bright cloud overshadowed them, and a voice from the cloud said, "This is my beloved Son, with whom I am well pleased; listen to him." When the disciples heard this, they fell on their faces, and were filled with awe. But Jesus came and touched them, saying, "Rise, and have no fear." And when they lifted up their eyes, they saw no one but Jesus only.
>
> Matt. 17:1-8

Less than a week after Peter's identification of Yeshua as the Messiah, the development of the symbol of the Christ and his kingdom reaches a startling zenith. Yeshua, Peter, James, and John climb a high mountain. Perhaps, it is Mt. Hermon or some other major peak of southern Lebanon. No matter, really. Far more important from a mythical point of view is that mountains have been used the world over to represent the *axis mundi* whereby heaven and earth are connected.[17] Even in the biblical tradition which emphasizes more than many others God's non-spatiality, Sinai functions as the locus for primary revelation. Later, Mount Carmel serves as the locale for a special revelation to Elijah, while the Temple is conceived of as being on a high mountain (Zion) even though, to the human eye, it is no more than a moderate-sized hill.

Just why men feel closer to the divine on mountains is a question which must be left to the psychologists of religion. In any event, it is to a high mountain that Yeshua quite deliberately takes his disciples. There, they receive a revelation comparable to the Sinaic revelation to Moses, a revelation which lifts the story of Yeshua into a wholly new plane. One could argue, indeed, that this is the central event in the whole Gospel narrative. To be sure, the disciples do not return to civilization with a new law code or set of inspired teachings. On the contrary, they are told to say nothing about what they have experienced. What they return with is the unspeakable, a dazzling vision of that light which, until this time, had only played gently around the fringes of their consciousness. This moment, then, totally refocuses the meaning of the title, Christos. The fact that each of the Synoptic Gospels follows the account of Peter's recognition with this story of the metamorphosis[18] of Yeshua indicates the close link between them.

While the four are alone on the mountain the human form which the light has been wearing incognito becomes transparent. Yeshua is transformed before their very eyes. His face radiates light as though he were the sun itself and his clothes become intensely white. The veil is torn asunder and that unearthly divine illumination of which John speaks at the beginning of his Gospel breaks forth. Most of us have seen hints—out of the corner of our eye, as it were—of the celestial light which plays about us continually. If man did not, religion would have died centuries ago. In Yeshua, this light is now focused intensely; what was intimated is now made clear.

As the light burns forth, synging the edges of the cosmos, human spatiality and temporality are suddenly abolished and

Yeshua is seen speaking with Moses, the lawgiver *par excellence*, and Elijah, the prototype of all prophets. Logos space transcends human space and the mountain becomes Sinai, Carmel—all mountains of revelation together. Logos time transcends all human time as Moses, Elijah, and Yeshua meet. The Logos light is now, present, ever here; perceived time is always then, gone, and dead. "Before Abraham was, I am," says Yeshua in another place (John 8:58). The moment of revelation on the mountain, be it to Moses or Elijah or the disciples, is always the same. It is not there but here; not then but now.

Peter, as usual, does not wholly understand. The mind of even the chief of the disciples cannot quite encompass this revelation. Hence, he suggests the building of three portable shrines, thus putting Yeshua on a par with Moses and Elijah and elevating all three to the rank of special holy saint if not god. From a human point of view his suggestion is understandable—but wrong. There are not three lights but one. The divine light which Yeshua has just revealed is the same light which called Moses and instructed Elijah. Even as Peter speaks, a cloud—the cloud of the Unknown—covers the mountain and the voice declares once more,

> This is my beloved Son, with whom I am well pleased;
> listen to him.

What then is the relationship between Yeshua and all those other pious and holy men of religion, the lawgivers and prophets of world history? Clearly, issofar as Yeshua is the transparent revelation of the light he alone must be attended. There are not many lights but one only. His absolute authority is to be found in that light. As such, He is the end (*telos*) toward which all the righteous have aimed. He reveals the law to Moses and God's word to Elijah. He is the pillar of cloud and fire which goes before Israel in the wilderness and the stone which, according to Rabbinic tradition and Paul, rolls behind them.[20]

At the same time, insofar as Moses and Elijah also indicate that light to men they are on a par with the man Yeshua. The authority is not in his visible manhood but in the light which that manhood reveals. In another place Yeshua says, "I am the Way, the Truth, and the Life; no one come to the Father, but by me."[21] Although

Christians have often used the text to justify their claim to sole possession of the truth, this is not necessarily the most obvious meaning. Rather, it would appear that Yeshua—speaking as the light—is saying that anyone who does come to the Father comes to him through the illuminating Logos. Thus the Winnebago Indian who calls upon the Great Spirit does so through the Logos. The words which Mohammed heard and wrote down as the Koran came from the Logos. The enlightenment of Gautama under the Bodhi tree comes through the Logos. In other words, in Yeshua one finds revealed that light which is the source of all illumination.[22] Yeshua is the light of the cosmos and it is that light which activates the inner eye of man to see the unseeable and know the unknowable. The revelation which Yeshua brings is not unique, particular, and Western but is absolutely universal. The Messiah is ruler of the cosmos.

The light, however, is always apprehended within a particular culture and at a particular time in the history of man. The tradition which develops in response to revelation must, by definition, take on a definite, historical form. When Peter saw Yeshua on the mountain he saw him with Moses and Elijah, not with Confucius and Lao-Tse. Revelation never takes place in a cacuum.

This means that although the light of Christ is universal, the Christian Church is not. Its symbols, doctrines, and traditions arose out of response to the light in the Greco-Roman and then primarily European world. It is a Western response to the Logos, not a purely universal response. Rather than trying to impose such Western cultural traditions upon others, the followers of the light ought first to open their eyes to the ways in which the light has already been revealed elsewhere. After all, the light which breaks forth under the Bodhi tree is, to use our Western term, *Christos*. So is the light which shimmers through the pases of the Tao Teh Ching, the *Bhagavad Gita*, and the Koran. There is no need to take Christ to the nations; he is already there.

This is not to say that there are not profound differences among the religions of mankind. Islam and Buddhism and Hinduism and Christianity surely do not agree about many issues. All of the various traditions have responded to the light in their own ways. All have also been profoundly corrupted over and over again by the darkness of the deluder. The ancient Jewish Pharisees whom Yeshua attacked had no monopoly on blindness. Repeatedly the ego manages to return to corrupt human belief and action. Nor does Christianity have any immunity to the temptations of the ego. From a neutral vantage point it would be difficult to argue that Christianity's testimony to the light is ultimately purer than that of mankind's other religions.

At the same time, it is fruitless to think that one can "get behind" all the religions of mankind and distill the essence of true religion. The essence of religion is unknowable, unimaginable, incomprehensible. As we have already said, *Theos* can only be spoken of negatively or mythologically. The first method simply cuts away the useless linguistic dross; the second method already presupposes a particular cultural tradition. The myth of the transfiguration of Yeshua is set within a Western Asian symbol system. No way exists to break out of that system to speak in purely universal terms. There is no need or purpose, then, in founding another new, universal religion. What men must do is to stop worrying about which tradition is the correct one and open their eyes to the light as it is attested to by their own tradition. Once it is apprehended there, it will be seen playing everywhere. Every tree in the backyard is potentially a Bodhi tree and a Cross.[23]

It may well be objected, however, that although "universalism" is attractive to many modern men, it is hardly to be found in the Bible. One is reminded of those repeated prophetic attacks upon the vanity of pagan religious practices and beliefs. Is not much of the Bible devoted to a wholesale rejection of idolatry?

Two responses need to be made to this obvious argument. The first is that the Bible is no more critical of pagan religions than it is of the religion of Israel itself. Repeatedly, it is "God's own people" who are subjected to the most virulent sort of criticism. Surely, this is also true in the New Testament where Roman centurions fare much better than Jewish scribes.

Second, the attack upon paganism in the Old Testament is limited in scope. Little is said about pagan mythology or doctrine.[24] Rather the prophets perennially attack either the notion that the created idol *is* itself the god it symbolizes or the practice of infusing religous practice with erotic desire. What is found wrong with non-Israelite (and Israelite) religion is the tendency to absolutize the myth and symbol at the expense of that toward which they point and to use such absolutized idols as props for the ego. The essential distinction, then, is not between the one right, Israelite, religion and all the wrong ones but between the children of light and children of darkness. False religion is religion which reads myth as but fact, confuses symbol and Suchness, and uses these indicators themselves as objects for erotic attachment. Even Yeshua, himself, when understood as a power toward which erotic desire for security is directed is an idol which must be destroyed. In order for the light to shine forth, the man Yeshua must die.

6

THE LAST THINGS

T he myth of the hero operates on several levels at once. While pointing always beyond himself to the unknown, the hero also acts out in the flesh the life of Everyman, revealing the Way which each of us must travel to salvation. Moreover, just as ontogeny repeats phylogeny, so the hero's life also intimates the way in which the final denouement of the cosmic drama which is being acted out before us will take place. The last days of Yeshua are both the last days of Everyman and the last days of the cosmos. Or, to put it another way, the myth of the eschaton is a myth which speaks of the end and the beginning of each person. From the point of view of the world and the ego, the last days are in the future; from the point of view of faith, they are *now*.

The four Gospels disagree about many details of the story—so many details, in fact, that no consistent biography of Yeshua can be written—but they all attest to the growing antagonism expressed by the world's authorities, Yeshua's final capture and trial, his suffering and death upon a cross, and his ultimate triumph over even that.

There have been many who have said that the whole meaning of the Gospel is to be found here, in Yeshua's death and resurrection. Hence, the creeds of the Church generally ignore his teaching and concentrate upon these central events.[1] If truth be told, however, once his death and resurrection are apprehended clearly, his teachings are understood and vice versa. There is no discrepancy between word and action. The passion[2] of Yeshua is the Sermon on the Mount.

I. The Last Entry

> And when they drew near to Jerusalem to Bethphage and Bethany, at the Mount of Olives, he sent two of his disciples, and said to them, "Go into the village opposite you, and immediately as you enter it you will find a colt tied on which no one has ever sat; untie it and bring it. If anyone says to you, "Why are you doing this?" say, "The Lord has need of it and will send it back here immediately." And they went away, and found a colt tied at the door out in the open street; and they untied it. And those who stood there said to them, "What are you doing, untying the colt?" And they told them what Jesus had said; and they let them go. And they brought the colt to Jesus, and they threw their garments on it; and he sat upon it. And many spread their garments on the road, and others spread leafy branches which they had cut from the fields. And those who went before and those who followed cried out, "Hosanna. Blessed is he who comes in the name of the Lord! Blessed is the kingdom of our father David that is coming! Hosanna in the highest!"
>
> Mark 11:1-11

All the Gospels agree that the last days begin with a triumphal entry. Yeshua, who makes his headquarters just east of Jerusalem, in the town of Bethany, chooses to enter the city riding as the Messiah was expected to appear, on a donkey.[3] Just in case the populace does not get that symbolic point, supporters precede and follow him shouting Messianic slogans. John claims that Yeshua so enters Jerusalem on a feast day but he does not specify which one. The use of palm branches would hint that it is Tabernacles (Succoth), but that is by no means certain.[4] All the Gospels, in any event, agree that whenever Yeshua enters, he enters as a king to be crowned. After recognition by the crowd, he proceeds directly to the Temple.

Why is it that Yeshua enters Jerusalem in this way at all? What purpose does his symbolic ride serve? Clearly he plans it carefully for some effect. Perhaps we can say that first and foremost it allows the crowds (and us) to see what Peter saw at Caesarea Philippi. It awakes in them the recognition of him as the Messiah, as the hope of Israel and the world. In effect, only after this recognition has been made can it be deepened and transformed by Yeshua's crucifixion. At the same time, this triumphal entry, made amidst shouting crowds and waving palms could do nothing less than bring Yeshua's conflict with the religious and political authorities to a head and hence produce the drama of the last days.

One thing is clear: Yeshua is not a pawn in the hands of fate, crucified merely by chance. At every moment he is thoroughly in control of the whole drama. He stimulates opposition among the rulers of the cosmos, encourages Judas to do what he must, waits long hours for his captors to arrive, and then does nothing to defend himself against the charges brought. At any moment he could work to save his ego, but he does not. He is determined to crucify that ego for the sake of the cosmos. Yeshua the king must die.

II. The Last Teachings

After recording his Messianic entry, Matthew and Mark picture Yeshua as staying near Jerusalem in Bethany so that he can teach every day in the Temple. Basically, his recorded sayings during this period concern either the refutation of religious authorities who seek to best him in argument or prophecies of the coming end and how to prepare for it. Among those passages recording disputes with the authorities two are of particular importance:

> 1. And they sent to him some of the Pharisees and some of the Herodians, to entrap him in his talk. And they came and said to him, "Teacher, we know that you are true, and care for no man; for you do not regard the position of men, but truly teach the way of God. Is it lawful to pay taxes to Caesar, or not? Should we pay them, or should we not?" But knowing their hypocrisy, he said to them, "Why put me to the test? Bring me a coin, and let me look at it." And they brought one. And he said to them, "Whose

likeness and inscription is this?" They said to him, "Caesar's." Jesus said to them, "Render to Caesar the things that are Caesar's, and to God the things that are God's." And they were amazed at him.

Mark 12:13-17

One of those perennial questions which reoccurs in human civilization is the question of the relation between religious commitment and civil authority. Concerning this matter, both the Jewish nationalists and the Romans were in theoretical agreement. That is, both sides believed that government and religion are inseparable. Thus Roman coins bore an inscription declaring Caesar "Deus" while Jewish nationalists yearned for the day when the Romans would be driven out and Israel could again be ruled according to God's Torah. In the meantime, while the Roman legions prevailed, Jews were made to compromise and make the best of a bad situation. A purist, unafraid of worldly authority, however, would refuse to pay Roman taxes which, after all, supported a pagan authority.

Yeshua, however, sees the matter differently, for to him both present Roman and possibly future Jewish governments are a part of the ever-changing illusory cosmos. Hence, he has no interest in leading a revolt against Roman authority. In fact, it was to be precisely such a revolt, carried out in the name of God, which led to the Jewish disaster in 70 A.D.[5]

The enlightened one has no interest in such human folly, except as it reveals to all the folly of man's imagination and egoism. Nationalism is but one more example of man's futile effort to secure himself against the flux of time. In Christ there are no ultimate distinctions between Jews and Romans. Hence Yeshua proves himself a most unusual Messiah. The Messiah who is expected to lead the zealots against the enemy refuses involvement. If the coin has Caesar's face on it, it must be his. Give it to him. It is no wonder that his hearers are amazed at him!

2. And Sadducees came to him, who say that there is no resurrection; and they asked him a question saying, "Teacher, Moses wrote for us that if a man's brother dies and leaves a wife, but leaves no child, the man must take the wife, and raise up children for his brother. There were seven brothers; the first took a

wife, and when he died left no children; and the second took her, and died, leaving no children; and the third likewise; and the seven left no children. Last of all the woman also died. In the resurrection whose wife will she be? For the seven had her as wife."

Jesus said to them, "Is not this why you are wrong, that you know neither the scriptures nor the power of God? For when they rise from the dead, they neither marry nor are given in marriage, but are like angels in heaven. And as for the dead being raised, have you not read in the book of Moses, in the passage about the bush how God said to him, 'I am the God of Abraham, and the God of Isaac, and the God of Jacob?' He is not God of the dead, but of the living; you are quite wrong.

Mark 12:18-27

Yeshua's conversation with the Sadducees is equally surprising. The Sadducees do not believe in the resurrection of the dead. Indeed, that bit of doubt is one of the hall marks of their tradition. To test Yeshua, they use an old chestnut about the woman who marries several men in turn. Whose wife will she then be at the resurrection?

Yeshua, in response, implies that marriage is an institution of this cosmos, which may be appropriate for this cosmos but which has nothing to do with the realm of light. In heaven, there is no distinction between male and female; in heaven, there are no marriages. Personal identity, the ego, is washed away and perishes. Men are, in heaven, like angels. Such questions, therefore, make no sense. They would only make sense if man's ego were somehow an imperishable substance which flies away to heaven at death or is raised in a new body. Neither is the case.[6]

On the other hand, Yeshua argues that even in the Torah Moses gives intimations of the resurrection—but hardly of the resurrection as it is normally conceived. Luke has Yeshua put it this way:

And Moses himself implies that the dead rise again, in the passage about the bush where he calls the Lord the God of Abraham, the God of Isaac, and the God of Jacob. Now he is God, not of the dead, but of the living, for to him all men are in fact alive.

Luke 20:37-38

That is to say, resurrection does not have to do with either the past or the future but with the present. All men are equally alive to God now, in the present. The resurrection is not so much something that will be as what *is*. Therefore, Yeshua says in John 11:25, "I *am* the resurrection." The raising of Lazarus from the dead is a finger pointing to what happens now. Resurrection is a waking up from the dream of the past to the Unknowable Present.

III. The Eschaton

And as he came out of the temple, one of his disciples said to him, "Look, Teacher, what wonderful stones and what wonderful buildings!" And Jesus said to him, "Do you see these great buildings? There will not be left here one stone upon another, that will not be thrown down."

And as he sat on the Mount of Olives opposite the temple, Peter and James and John and Andrew asked him privately, "Tell us, when will this be, and what will be the sign when these things are all to be accomplished?" And Jesus began to say to them, "Take heed that no one leads you astray. Many will come in my name, saying, 'I am he!' and they will lead many astray. And when you hear of wars and rumors of wars, do not be alarmed; this must take place, but the end is not yet. For nation will rise against nation, and kingdom against kingdom; there will be earthquakes in various places, there will be famines; this is but the beginning of the sufferings.

"But take heed to yourselves; for they will beliver you up to councils; and you will be beaten in synagogues; and you will stand before governors and kings for my sake, to bear testimony before them. And the gospel must first be preached to all nations. And the gospel must first be preached to all nations. And when they bring you to trial and deliver you up, do not be anxious beforehand what you are to say; but say whatever is given you in that hour, for it is not you who speak, but the Holy Spirit. And brother will deliver up brother to death and the father his child and children will rise against parents and have them put to death; and you will be hated by all for my name sake. But he who endures to the end will be saved.

"But when you see the desolating sacrilege set up where it ought not to be (let the reader understand), then let those who are in Judea flee to the mountains; let him who is on the housetop not go down, nor enter his house to take anything away; and let him who is in the field not turn back to take his mantle. And alas for those who are with child and for those who give suck in those days! Pray that it may not happen in winter. For in those days there will be such tribulation as has not been from the beginning of the creation which God created until now, and never will be. And if the Lord had not shortened the days, no human being would be saved; but for the sake of the elect, when he chose, he shortened the days. And then if any one says to you, 'Look, here is the Christ!' or 'Look, there he is!' do not believe it. False Christs and false prophets will arise and show signs and wonders, to lead astray, if possible, the elect. But take heed; I have told you all things beforehand.

"But in those days, after that tribulation, the sun will be darkened, and the moon will not give its light, and the stars will be falling from heaven, and the powers in the heavens will be shaken. And then they will see the Son of Man coming in clouds with great power and glory. And then he will send out the angels and gather his elect from the four winds, from the ends of the earth to the ends of heaven."

Mark 13:1-27

Just as myths of creation are a projection into the distant past of the truth of the present, so myths of the eschaton project into the future a vision of the world's ephemerality and illusoriness. Not only the Temple, that human model of the cosmos which stands as a link to the divine on the highest of all mountains, but even the sun, moon, and stars will eventually be destroyed. What seems now so permanent and secure will fall apart at the seams. The reel of the cosmos will eventually be wholly unwound and the true light will shine through in all its glory.

Needless to say, there is no sense that this culmination will take place because of some general progress toward the light on the part of man. The world is the domain of the ego and hence will always be filled with conflict, bitterness, and pain. There will always be wars and rumors of wars, famine, disease, and brutality, because the imagination of man invariably causes them. No self-styled Messiah could possibly help the situation, for such Messiahs are inevitably part of the problem, not the answer. Even if some son of David were to defeat the Romans decisively, organize a large and prosperous Jewish state, and lay down the most judicious and equitable of laws, the world would remain the world. The cosmos and each individual in it, therefore, must wait with hope for the coming of the Son of Man.

When one translates this myth back into more individual terms it means this: All men are, at root, the divine light which John calls logos, but all are also bound in those webs of illusion which we call the ego-world. No ego can break the bonds of illusion, for the ego itself is the problem. Hence, the inner eye can only be opened by that which is beyond the world and of which we cannot really speak.

At the same time, although nothing can cause revelation to occur, Yeshua does provide us with certain ways of preparation which Matthew includes in Chapters 24 and 25 of his Gospel. Basically, the guidelines are these:

a. Stay alert. (Matt. 24:37-44, 25:1-13) Expect the unexpected. Do not assume that you have forever to prepare, for the unprepared shall not enter the kingdom.

b. Treat your fellowmen as children of light, as Christ. (26:31-46) See in each person in need—the stranger, the thirsty, the hungry—a reflection of the divine light. Know that when the light comes, good treatment of your fellow men will be very important. (24:45-51)

c. Make use of what you have been given. (25:14-30) Do not lament the absence of the Master; maximize the talents of gold which are entrusted to you. No man is totally without the light; try to see as much as you can. If you do not exercise your inner eye, the light will never dawn and you will surely be filled with darkness.

The coming of the Son of Man, is, of course, a two-edged sword. For those totally caught up in the web of the ego, his advent is a shattering, destructive experience. It is the apprehension of our familiar world, which finds its center and focus in the ego, being swept away. The myth of the judgment day is the portrayal of the world's ephemerality and meaninglessness, a vision of absolute panic and horror. Only those who have prepared for the coming of the Master and who indeed know themselves to be thoroughly one with him can find solace in his epiphany. No one can create that moment through any sort of meditation or discipline. But preparation is nevertheless necessary. Without it the coming of the light can only shatter and destroy.

IV. The Last Supper

And on the first day of the Unleavened Bread, when they sacrificed the passover lamb, the disciples said to him, "Where will you have us go and prepare for you to eat the passover?" And he sent two of his disciples, and said to them, "Go into the city, and a man carrying a jar of water will meet you; follow him, and wherever he enters, say to the householders, "The Teacher says, 'Where is my guest room, where I am to eat the passover with my disciples?' And he will show you a large upper room furnished and ready; there prepare for us." And the disciples set out and went to the city, and found it as he had told them; and they prepared the passover.

And when it was evening he came with the twelve. And as they were at table eating, Jesus said, "Truly, I say to you, one of you will betray me, one who is eating with me." They began to be sorrowful, and to say to him one after another, "Is it I?" He said to them, "It is one of the twelve, one who is dipping bread in the same dish with me. For the Son of man goes as it is written of him, but woe to that man by whom the Son of man is betrayed! It would have been better for that man if he had not been born."

And as they were eating, he took bread, and blessed, and broke it, and gave it to them, and said, "Take; this is my body." And he took a cup, and when he had given thanks he gave it to them, and they all drank of it. And he said to them, "This is my blood of the covenant, which is poured out for many. Truly, I say to you, I shall not drink again of the fruit of the vine until that day when I drink it new in the Kingdom of God."

And when they had sung a hymn, they went out to the Mount of Olives.

Mark 14:12-26

There are few passages in either the Old or New Testaments more important for the development of Christian worship than the Gospel accounts of the Last Supper. One could argue cogently that at root the action here described defines what such worship is and how it is structured. That is, the center of worship from the beginning of the Church has been the eating of the bread and the drinking of wine, accompanied by Yeshua's words of institution.

What is a liturgical cornerstone, however, turns out to be also an historical nightmare. All four gospels do agree that there was a Last Supper at which Yeshua made clear his awareness of his betrayal by one of the disciples, but that is about where universal agreement ends. John (13:1ff) dates the supper on the Day of Preparation, the day preceding Passover itself. Although he identifies Yeshua as the true vine (15:1ff), he mentions nothing about the institution of the Lord's Supper. Instead, he describes in some detail Yeshua's commendation of the practice of foot-washing.

The Synoptics, on the other hand, identify the Last Supper as the Passover meal and include Yeshua's words of institution. In other words, for the first three Gospels, the Last Supper is, in origin, a Seder service when Israel celebrates her salvation in the land of Egypt. There are, however, several points of disagreement even among the Synoptics. Luke, for instance, places the blessing of the cup before the breaking of the bread. Nowhere does he identify the wine as the blood of Yeshua. Luke also includes the account of a dispute among the disciples (concerning which follower is greatest) which the others omit. (Luke 22:24-30) Like John, but unlike Matthew and Mark he includes Yeshua's prediction of Peter's denial within the account of the supper itself. Also unlike the other Synoptics Luke overtly connects the breaking of the bread and the betrayal of Judas.

Matthew and Mark are most alike, but even between them there is one major difference: while Mark has Yeshua say, "This is my blood of the covenant, which is poured out for many," Matthew adds, "for the remission of sins." Clearly, in these two gospels the text is so worded that it may be used easily as a liturgical formula within the context of worship. All extraneous, historical references have been removed so that the reader can concentrate upon those central words of Yeshua.

When one examines with care all the variations to be found in the tradition, historical reconstruction of what actually happened at the supper seems difficult, if not impossible. From our point of view, however, such an historical reconstruction would be irrelevant anyway. The question is not what actually happened, but what the myth itself means. We must simply take the story as the Gospels present it without worrying about historical considerations. This does not mean, however, that our task has been made simple, for the essential question remains. We are still left with those peculiar sayings of Jesus which have stuck in Christian minds throughout the centuries:

This is my body, (and) This is my blood.

The more one turns them over in the mind, the stranger and more unaccountable they become. Theologians and church historians have tried to ease our burden by offering theological explanations and historical reconstructions, but we must not imbibe too quickly of such pain-killing nerve tonics. Rather, we must wrestle with such sayings for ourselves and by ourselves.

What can Yeshua mean when he takes bread and blesses and breaks it and says, "This is my body." How can Yeshua speak of the bread as his body when he stands before us in the flesh? To be sure, *estin* (is) can be translated without too much stretching "symbolizes", but does that solve anything? Why does Yeshua want his disciples to act symbolically like cannibals? Why doesn't he say, "This is my spirit given for you"? What is Yeshua's specific relation to his body and the bread? To whom or what does the pronoun "my" refer?

A host of similar questions bubbles up in connection with the "blood" sayings. Why does Yeshua ask his disciples to drink his blood when the Jewish tradition forbids the drinking of even animal blood?[7] And what is the covenant which this blood represents? This is the only time in any of the four gospels that Yeshua so much as mentions the word "covenant". Why does he suddenly introduce it here? And who are the many for whom the blood will be poured forth.

In all three Synoptics Yeshua says something to the effect that he will not drink again of the fruit of the vine until the kingdom of God comes. What does he really mean by that? Does he believe that the kingdom of God is soon to become a tangible, political reality? What is the relation between our drinking of the wine with the disciples and the kingdom?

The more one looks at this passage, the more one is aware that at the very heart of Christian worship is an enigma wrapped in mystery. Whether one approaches the subject from an historical or a psychological or a theological point of view one runs almost immediately into a stone wall constructed of question marks. Innumerable answers to these questions have been given but, as might be predicted, they reflect as much about the answerer as they do about the question.

Like Alexander the Great before the Gordian knot, most of us can not abide complicated conundrums for long. Therefore in each age, the sword of explanation is soon drawn to slice through the difficulties. Sometimes the explanation is philosophical, sometimes historical. Some have retreated to emotive meaning.

If we are honest, however, we must admit that the knot remains. Yeshua returns once more to announce as enigmatically as ever, "This is my body; this is my blood." And we are bound to jettison all those old solutions and try once more.

The more one struggles with these words honestly, the more one recognizes that they are like a diamond bit which grinds away everything it touches. Under their pressure both historical common sense and philosophical reason dissolve into heaps of fine dust which are blown away by the wind. We find, indeed, that the words bore into the ego itself, destroying the barrier between something and no thing, opening a fissure through which light can break forth.

Explanations seek to remove all paradoxical tensions; yet it is precisely such tensions which give these words power. Both philosophical and historical approaches are ways through which the ego protects itself from the devastating power of these words.

Understanding emerges only when the diamond cutter has been allowed to do its work.[8]

V. The Last Judgment

And they went to a place which was called Gethsemane; and he said to his disciples, "Sit here, while I pray." And he took with him Peter and James and John, and began to be greatly distressed and troubled. And he said to them, "My soul is very sorrowful, even to death; remain here, and watch." And going a little farther, he fell on the ground and prayed that, if it were possible, the hour might pass from him. And he said, "Abba, Father, all things are possible to thee; remove this cup from me; yet not what I will, but what thou wilt." And he came and found them sleeping, and he said to Peter, "Simon, are you asleep? Could you not watch one hour? Watch and pray that you may not enter into temptation; the spirit indeed is willing, but the flesh is weak." And again he went away and prayed, saying the same words. And again he came and found them sleeping, for their eyes were very heavy; and they did not know what to answer him. And he came the third time, and said to them, "Are you still sleeping and taking your rest? It is enough; the hour has come; the Son of man is betrayed into the hands of sinners. Rise, let us be going; see, my betrayer is at hand."

And immediately, while he was still speaking, Judas came, one of the twelve, and with him a crowd with swords and clubs, from the chief priests and the scribes and the elders. Now the betrayer had given them a sign, saying, "The one I shall kiss is the man; seize him and lead him away safely." And when he came, he went up to him at once, and said, "Master!" And kissed him. And they laid hands on him and seized him. But one of those who stood by drew his sword, and struck the slave of the high priest and cut off his ear. And Jesus said to them, "Have you come out as against a robber, with swords and clubs to capture me? Day after day I was with you in the temple teaching, and you did not seize me. But let the scriptures be fulfilled." And they all forsook him, and fled.

And a young man followed him, with nothing but a linen cloth about his body; and they seized him, but he left the linen cloth and ran away naked.

And they led Jesus to the high priest; and all the chief priests and the elders and the scribes were assembled. And Peter had followed him at a distance, right into the courtyard of the high priest; and he was sitting with the guards, and warming himself at the fire. Now the chief priests and the whole council sought testimony against Jesus to put him to death; but they found none. For many bore false witness against him, and their witness did not agree. And some stood up and bore false witness against him, saying, "We heard him say, 'I will destroy this temple that is made with hands, and in three days I will build another, not made with hands.' " Yet not even so did their testimony agree. And the high priest stood up in the midst, and asked Jesus, "Have you no answer to make? What is it that these men testify against you?" But he was silent and made no answer. Again the high priest asked him, "Are you the Christ, the Son of the Blessed?" And Jesus said, "I am; and you will see the Son of man sitting at the right hand of Power, and coming with the clouds of heaven." And the high priest tore his mantle, and said, "Why do we still need witnesses? You have heard his blasphemy. What is your decision?" And they all condemned him as deserving death. And some began to spit on him, and to cover his face, and to strike him, saying to him, "Prophesy!" And the guards received him with blows.

And as Peter was below in the courtyard, one of the maids of the high priest came; and seeing Peter warming himself, she looked at him, and said, "You also were with the Nazrene, Jesus." But he denied it, saying, "I neither know nor understand what you mean." And he went out into the gateway. And the maid saw him, and began again to say to the bystanders, "This man is one of them; for you are a Galilean." But he began to invoke a curse on himself and to swear. "I do not know this man of whom you speak." And immediately the cock crowed a second time. And Peter remembered how Jesus had said to him, "Before the cock crows twice, you will deny me three times." And he broke down and wept.

And as soon as it was morning the chief priests, with the elders and scribes, and the whole council held a consultation; and they bound Jesus and led him away and delivered him to Pilate. And Pilate asked him, "Are you the King of the Jews?" And he answered him, "You have said so." And the chief priests accused him of many things. And Pilate again asked him, "Have you no answer to make? See how many charges they bring against you." But Jesus made no further answer, so that Pilate wondered.

Now at the feast he used to release for them one prisoner whom they asked. And among the rebels in prison, who had committed murder and insurrection, there was a man called Barabbas. And the crowd came up and began to ask Pilate to do as he was wont to do for them. And he answered them, "Do you want me to release for you the King of the Jews?" For he perceived that it was out of envy that the chief priests had delivered him up. But the chief priests stirred up the crowd to have him release for them Barabbas instead. And Pilate again said to them, "Then what shall I do with the man whom you call the King of the Jews?" And they cried out again, "Crucify him." And Pilate said to them, "Why, what evil has he done?" But they said all the more, "Crucify him." So Pilate, wishing to satisfy the crowd, released for them Barabbas; and having scourged Jesus, he delivered him to be crucified.

And the soldiers led him away inside the palace (that is, the praetorium); and they called together the whole battalion. And they clothed him in a purple cloak, and plaiting a crown of thorns they put it on him. And they began to salute him, "Hail, King of the Jews!" And they struck his head with a reed, and spat upon him, and they knelt down in homage to him. And when they had mocked him, they stripped him of the purple cloak, and put his own clothes on him. And they led him out to crucify him.

And they compelled a passer-by, Simon of Cyrene,

who was coming in from the country, the father of Alexander and Rufus, to carry his cross. And they brought him to the place called Golgotha (which means the place of a skull). And they offered him wine mingled with myrrh; but he did not take it. And they crucified him, and divided his garments among them, casting lots for them, to decide what each should take. And it was the third hour, when they crucified him. And the inscription of the charge against him read, "The King of the Jews." And with him they crucified two robbers, one on his right and one on his left. And those who passed by derided him, wagging their heads, and saying, "Aha! You who would destroy the temple and build it in three days, save yourself, and come down from the cross!" So also the chief priests mocked him to one another with the scribes, saying, "He saved others; he cannot save himself. Let the Christ, the King of Israel, come down now from the cross, that we may see and believe." Those who were crucified with him also reviled him.

And when the sixth hour had come, there was darkness over the whole land until the ninth hour. And at the ninth hour Jesus cried with a loud voice, "E'lo-i, E'lo-i, la'ma sabach-tha'ni?" which means, "My God, my God, why hast thou forsaken me?" And some of the bystanders hearing it said, "Behold, he is calling Elijah." And one ran and, filling a sponge full of vinegar, put it on a reed and gave it to him to drink, saying, "Wait, let us see whether Elijah will come to take him down." And Jesus uttered a loud cry, and breathed his last. And the curtain of the temple was torn in two, from top to bottom. And when the centurion, who stood facing him, saw that he thus breathed his last, he said, "Truly this man was the Son of God!"

There were also women looking on from afar, among whom were Mary Magdalene, and Mary the mother of James the younger and of Joses, and Salome, who, when he was in Galilee, followed him, and ministered to him; and also many other women who came up with him to Jerusalem.

And when evening had come, since it was the day of Preparation, that is, the day before the sabbath, Joseph of Arimathea, a respected member of the council, who was also himself looking for the kingdom of God, took courage and went to Pilate, and asked for the body of Jesus. And Pilate wondered if he were already dead; and summoning the centurion, he asked him whether he was already dead. And when he learned from the centurion that he was dead, he granted the body to Joseph. And he bought a linen shroud, and taking him down, wrapped him in the linen shroud, and laid him in a tomb which had been hewn out of the rock; and he rolled a stone against the door of the tomb. Mary Magdalene and Mary the mother of Joses saw where he was laid.

Mark 14:32-15:47

The moment in which all other moments finding their meaning is finally upon us. The world of egoistic darkness can no longer abide the presence of the light in its midst and conspires to snuff it out. The religious authorities, intent upon preserving their traditions against the threat of time and change, find the light blasphemous and threatening and hence deny their own Law in order to condemn it. The civil authority cannot stand the threats of the egoistic mob and, as a consequence, denies its own canons of justice. The disciples, fearful lest they too be destroyed, aid and abet the world. Even Yeshua's own psyche resists, sadly, its coming demise. [9]

This, then, is no struggle between the righteous and the unrighteous. There are, in this drama, no good men, for all betray and fall away at the last. Caiaphas, Pilate, Judas, and Peter are all part and parcel of the world of the ego and as such struggle violently against the light. Therefore, the victory which emerges is not a victory of one group over another. In Yeshua's triumph, Christians certainly do not reveal their superiority over Jews. Rather, the victory is the victory of life over death, of man over his own corpse. Man breaks forth from the chains of bondage; the power of the ego is overcome.

In the midst of this company of the unjust which constitutes the cast of characters, the light itself shines steadily, unwavering in its luminosity. Each actor seems to work for the destruction of the light; yet it is the light which is behind everything. The more the authorities rage, the more they reveal the light's power and the closer the light's victory comes. It is the world itself, in all its egotistical darkness which makes the triumph, after all, possible.

The stage is full of ironies. Disciples fall asleep at the moment of crisis; religious leaders who purport to teach the truth of God do not recognize him standing before them; Pontius Pilate, whose vocation is justice, tries to protect Yeshua but in so doing destroys justice completely. And Yeshua, the one man who ought to be protecting himself by offering sound defense says nothing except words which would sound blasphemous to any orthodox ears.

The world is turned inside out in this, the strangest of all trials. This is the very obverse of the myth of the Hydra. In that myth man is confronted by the Hydra as enemy and seeks victory by lopping off its head. With each blow, however, new heads are born and the situation becomes increasingly threatening. This is the myth of the ego seeking to solve its own problems and in so doing creating more and more of them. It is, in fact, the story of man.

In the Yeshua myth the hero does nothing but allow the enemy to do its worst. By doing nothing, the hero triumphs over the most subtle enemy of all—himself. Long ago, Lao-tse said, "The sage accomplishes without any action."[10] From the point of view of the ego and common sense, this isn't really true. In our world of imaginative fantasy, nothing gets done without effort. Therefore, we believe that the victory of light over darkness must also take supreme effort. I want a plan, formula, method by which I can achieve salvation. In truth, however, I will never achieve for I am the problem from which the light saves. The more effort I make, the worse the situation becomes. Therefore Yeshua stands before us doing nothing.

At last, the decision is made; the cross is carried; the nails are hammered. Darkness falls upon the earth and we can see. Good and evil have joined hands. The best and the worst are revealed as indistinguishable. The world does its worst by driving out and destroying the light which it cannot abide; yet in so doing does its very best. Yeshua hangs on the Tree of Death—and Life—as a revelation of one awful fact: Death and Life are one. There is no distinction between them. "He who would save his life shall lose it, but he who would lose his life for my sake shall find it."

Once upon a time, a long, long time ago, man ate of the tree of knowledge of good and evil and since that time has lived under the shade of its branches.[11] There everything has been good or bad, righteous or unrighteous, Godly or demonic. Men, especially the "best" men, have spent their lives making such weighty distinctions. Yeshua, in his heroic struggle, lays his axe to the root of that old tree so that a new shoot, the shoot of the Tree of Life may emerge. This strange tree, with its two branches fashioned to support the weight of dying man, offers no shade at all. All it provides is a place to hang painfully under the searing heat of the noonday sun. Compared to the tree of good and evil it appears ominously stark and foreboding. And yet . . . and yet, in its ugliness it offers man's only hope. In its Death it is the Tree of Life.

7

RESURRECTION: BEYOND THE END

And when the sabbath was past, Mary Magdalene, and Mary the mother of James, and Salome, bought spices, so that they might go and anoint him. And very early on the first day of the week they went to the tomb when the sun had risen. And they were saying to one another, "Who will roll away the stone for us from the door of the tomb?" And looking up, they saw that the stone was rolled back; for it was very large. And entering the tomb, they saw a young man sitting on the right side, dressed in a white robe; and they were amazed. And he said to them, "Do not be amazed; you seek Jesus of Nazareth, who was crucified. He has risen, he is not here; see the place where they laid him. But go, tell his disciples and Peter that he is going before you to Galilee; there you will see him, as he told you."

Mark 16:1-8

T he hero has at last performed his supreme task, a task which makes the cleansing of the Augean stables or the defeat of the fire drake look like mere child's play. He has, like the miraculous caterpillar, entered the cocoon of death so that the butterfly of life may emerge. He has shed the past and dead to live in the present.

The resurrection must always be thought of in the present. "I *am* the resurrection," says Yeshua. Only mythical license allows projection into the past or future. Other events may have happened, but the resurrection is now. Christ emerges from the grave as the Now man, as that which makes all things possible, as the light of the world. The Risen One is living witness to the "I am" which emerges when our grip upon the old man is released. This is no mere sign or promise of life after death and the grave. The resurrection is not after anything. The resurrection is now; it is the hub upon which the circle of time turns. Ego time is past and future. The ego wants to know what will happen next. The resurrection is not next, for the resurrection does not occur. The resurrection *is*.

Yeshua's return in the flesh is not just a sign of our future resurrection, at least not in the individualistic way we normally think. In the world we are many, with individual distinctions and differences. But the light is one and all men are one in that light. In Christ Everyman is illumined; Everyman is raised. He is not the image of what everyone ought to be but of what everyone is.

To be sure, Yeshua returns in the flesh with his own particular characteristics and wounds. The nail holes and the slashed side are very much in evidence. A body is really there. But it is the body of "I am", not the ego.[1] The wounds which he bears are wounds which are characteristic of Man. Yeshua's resurrected body reveals that the other side to which he has crossed and this side are not separated by an impassible gulf. Life in the Christ is not escape from the cosmos but its affirmation. The Now Man can live in the body in this world.

In his death and resurrection, Yeshua indicates the narrow defile through which man must pass on his way from Death to Life. We, however, stare at this way in amazement, for it is a way which is no way at all. Who or what can it be which passes over? The ego? No, for it is the ego which must be left behind; Yeshua must die. The Light? No, for the light has no need to pass over. The light is the light and has no need for illumination.

What then has happened? Nothing—and everything. Nothing, because all that can happen, happens in this cosmos, in this realm of time and space and ego. A man has been crucified and that in itself is but an example of the finitude and impermanence of the cosmos. Every ego perishes forever. No light can enter the realm of the ego for the ego is the prince of darkness, the ruler of the dead. Beyond the demise of the ego there can be NOTHING.

But that Nothing is everything. The darkness has fled before the light of day. The Son of Adam, the New Man, rises from the tomb of Yeshua. He *is* Yeshua, though many do not recognize him as such immediately. He stands forth as light in the midst of darkness, as the other Unspeakable and Unknowable One made visible.

Just as Yeshua during his days on earth revealed to those with eyes to see the light which is Logos, so the One which arises is the light focused in Yeshua's marred and wounded body. They are one. Death has been rendered no death at all. There is no death; the cataclysmic crossing is no crossing whatsoever.

From a common human vantage point there is but one world, the world of the ego, sense-perception, things. In so far as supernatural beings exist they are part of the world of differentiation. I am one thing, God is something else. The Enlightened One, however, points to that other Unknown and Unknowable realm—the kingdom of God, *Brahman, Dharmakaya* — which transcends the changeable, suffering world of illusion. Now one may distinguish between illusion and that ever-glowing timeless light named "I am." The problem is: how does one leave the realm of the ego behind and enter the realm of light?

The Risen One reveals this to be no question at all. The two worlds are one. There is no great divide, no crossing, no experience of enlightenment.[2] There is only the light. How could anyone experience Enlightenment? It is the ego which wants experiences. How could any one enter the realm of light when that realm is no spatialized thing to be entered? How could the inner eye be activated when there is no thing for it to see?

Clearly we have arrived at the beginning of our quest. The myth of Yeshua, like the myth of Gautama, points toward that unspeakable, unrealized unknown upon which the whole of the cosmos depends and which we are. In the end the myth erases itself and we are left with nothing, *nirvana*.

So then does the world end with a whimper, not a bang? Are we left only with the dissolution of an illusory world and the mystery of unspeakable nothingness? Is the end of the story but a mystic blur as many suspected anyway? Hardly, for neither resurrection nor *nirvana* is a denial of life.[2] Rather they are an affirmation of what makes life possible. Yeshua returns from the death of the ego in the flesh, in this cosmos, for mankind. And from the Nothingness which is All bubble forth the waters of agape which flow, like the four rivers out of Eden, to fertilize the earth.

Agape knows no distinctions among men, for it springs from the knowledge that all men are One. There are no enemies who are beyond the pale. Even the most vicious killer is, at root, the One who is called Christ. Even the most pious saint is also an example of that illusory ego called Satan. Thus agape treats all with an even hand.

Agape is concerned about human needs and reaches out to the hungry, the thirsty, to those who are naked, lest such needs blind men to the light. At the same time, agape is not in the business of propping up egos with the securities of this world. The risen Christ, therefore, calls the disciples, not to social action programs, but to baptism. Only as the old man is drowned in the flood waters of death can the New Man emerge victorious. Charity which considers man's happiest state as one of affluence is no charity at all.

Clearly, many will object to this, for our common sense tells us that what man needs are the things a new governmental program can provide. And surely one must take care lest the position outlined above be used as a rationalization for man's lack of concern for his neighbor's welfare. Still, one searches in vain in the New Testament for anything resembling a plan for social reform. The poor, says Yeshua, are always with us (Mark 14:7) and care should certainly be taken of them. What faith specifically demands, however, is the preaching of the good news and the baptism of the nations.

At the same time, when the axe of the gospel strikes at the root of both personal and corporate illusion, it strikes at the root of social injustice, prejudice and enmity as well. As long as men believe in the ego as their ultimate reality, as long as men accept such fantasies as nations, money, and military power as "real", no program of social action can do more than shift the locus for injustice. While eros prevails, justice can be little more than a balancing of the power of various interest groups. In that situation, minorities are bound to lose.

There is a place, of course, for "provisional ethics," e.e., for ethics which recognize the blindness of man, his erotic attachments, and hence the inevitability of injustice. Such ethics seek to make the best out of a bad situation by muting the most vicious forms of human egotism. One should not confuse such necessary attempts to confine human illusions within bounds, however, with the teachings of Yeshua. The Gospel not only recognizes sin but constitutes a wholesale attack upon it. The resurrection is a sign of victory over egotistical illusion, not merely the forgiveness of it.

Disciples, as Yeshua points out repeatedly, should only expect to be forgiven in so far as they forgive. Forgiveness, like judgment, conforms to the causal laws of *karma*. The meaning of the resurrection is not unmitigated forgiveness, but triumph. The old man shall always perish; forgiveness of him makes no sense, for he is the power of Satan itself. The New Man, on the other hand, needs no forgiveness; he is the power of the Enlightening One who triumphs in the resurrection.

To be sure, an understanding of the world as an illusory projection and the severing of the erotic bonds of desire do prompt an attitude of total acceptance. The illumined one can forgive 70x7 times, for he no longer has to defend his old ego. Such forgiveness is absolute, not partial. Ultimately, one cannot distinguish between the impressively pious man and the most vicious criminal, for they both are a part of the cosmos; both must be accepted for what they are—the Son of God. Therefore, if someone hits you on the cheek, turn the other one. To do otherwise would be to fall prey to the ego and its snares.

Much more might be said about the resurrection and its meaning, but already we tread upon dangerous territory. Essentially the illumined life is not a theory but a process. The myth of Yeshua must be lived through, not theorized about. The balm of the resurrection will only heal after the sword of the gospel has done its bloody work. To proclaim preemptorily that the resurrection signals a new acceptance of the world and the ego is dangerous unless the warfare against the old deluder has already run its course.

One ought not to read through to the end of the Gospels too quickly but should linger with the other truths which precede the resurrection until they are mastered. The crucifixion of the old Adam must take place before the resurrection of the New Adam can be accomplished. The gospel is not a position but a Way. Nothing in what has been said should be construed as having anything to do with metaphysical or ontological or psychological theory.

Ultimately, then, this book is highly dangerous and must be read very circumspectly. The seeker of illumination needs, not an overview such as is provided here but a Master who will indicate the direction of the Way step-by-step. The struggle against the deluder will be won, not by general theories but by well-aimed, specific blows.

Unfortunately, the Master-disciple relation, which looms so large in the New Testament, has been largely discarded by the Church. Theoretical theologians and canon lawyers are legion; spiritual Rabbis are few. Hence the path is largely untrod. Theological students are encouraged to become historiographers and/or philosophers rather than pilgrims. The inner eye remains closed.

A disciple must take upon himself the discipline of Yeshua; yet this is no set of laws or doctrines which can be encompassed in a book. The Way has little to do with rules and dogmas. The Early Church was at least partially correct in this: it depended primarily upon a succession of apostolic teachers for the preservation of the church. Presumably such teachers did not purvey general theories but advised their disciples concerning effective ways to engage the old deluder in mortal combat.

Therefore, all readers who have persevered this far are strongly urged to take what has been said with a grain of salt. The disciple must engage in battle, not just theorize about the nature of war. This book will only have performed its task if it has facilitated that first step along the Way. If it leads the reader to say, "Oh now I understand," it has failed miserably.

And so we come to the end of this mythological essay. Whether we have said something or nothing I leave to the reader to determine. But let us not make claims too grandiose. At most mythology has been written about a myth, a mythology which is

115

no closer to univocal language about *Theos* than the Gospels themselves. It is a mythology which, once heard, should be immediately erased. Certainly let us hope that it does not become dogma, even for a few. Theology is a reflex action, an absurd attempt to express the inexpressible. Now that that refles has been activated and theology has emerged, it is time once more to be silent.

NOTES

PREFACE

1. The term is taken from Aldous Huxley, *The Perennial Philosophy* (New York: Harper and Bros., 1945).

   It should be emphasized that one must exercise more care than Huxley does in distinguishing among such traditions as Hinduism, Buddhism, and Taoism. Although it must be admitted that they share many ideas in common, they do not teach the same philosophy. In order to avoid extensive discussions about the differences among those traditions, this volume is keyed to Mahayana Buddhism.

1. THEOS: A PROLEGOMENA

1. *Theos*, which is usually translated God, is left here in its original Greek form to indicate that the reader should not apply the usual connotations of "God" to it. That is, one must distinguish between God as a character in the mythological drama and *Theos* as that Unknown toward which myths point. Within the Christian myth, God the Father has several definable, personal characteristics. He speaks from heaven. he loves, he judges, etc. *Theos*, on the other

hand, is neither personal nor impersonal, neither passionate nor apathetic, either existent nor non-existent.

2. *Logoi* is simply the plural form of logos from which is derived the common suffix—ology.

3. In so far as history is defined as the study of the past, all human knowledge is historical. Such knowledge is also considered scientific to the extent that it is assumed that tomorrow's phenomena will operate according to the same laws which are found to be operating today. Such an assumption has proved to be highly useful but it must be observed that it may also be misleading when dealing with extensive periods of time.

4. Metaphysics means, literally, "after or beyond the physics." That is, after one has examined nature one can derive from it certain abstract generalizations and concepts. Ontology, a word sometimes taken to be synonymous with metaphysics, means "the study of being."

5. Thomas Aquinas identified God with the principle of the Unmoved Mover postulated by Aristotle. Duns Scotus quite acutely observed, however, that if one begins with physical motion and then traces such motion back to its cause, that cause must, by definition, also be physical.

Paul Tillich is probably the best known modern theologian to identify God with Being (or, when pressed too hard on that subject, with the Ground of Being). Paul Tillich, *Systematic Theology*, 3 Vols, (Chicago: University of Chicago Press, 1950, 1957, 1963), I, 163-286.

6. A. J. Ayer, *Language, Truth, and Logic* (New York: Dover Publications, n.d.), pp. 114-120.

7. Cf. Edward Conze, *Buddhist Scriptures* (Baltimore: Penguin Books, 1973), pp. 149-151.

8. Immanuel Kant, in the 18th Century, based his so-called Copernican revolution in philosophy upon the observation that in our perception it is the mind itself which structures the world spatially, temporally, and causally. We see quantitatively because the mind is structured quantitatively; we see causally because the mind is structured causally. Kant, however, generally assumed that all minds structure the world in the same way. This is an assumption which, under scrutiny, does not seem to hold up.

Buddhist philosophers had performed this same revolution centuries before Kant. It is true that such philosophers (one thinks particularly of early Mahayana thinkers like Ashvagosha, Nagarjuna, Asanga, and Vasabandu) began with quite different assumptions, for their aim was to justify intellectually the notions of *samsara* and *anatta* rather than, like Kant, to resolve certain problems raised by Newtonian science. Still, their conclusions are similar: one cannot think of the world apart from the structure provided for it by mind. There is no world apart from mind. Cf. T. R. V. Murti, *The Central Philosophy of Buddhism* (London: George Allen and Unwin Ltd., 1960), pp. 293-301; and D. T. Suzuki, *Outlines of Mahayana Buddhism* (New York: Schocken Books, 1967), pp. 87-98.

9. Actually, since "source" is a concept derived from the world of cause and effect, it can only be applied metaphorically to Nothing. Univocally nothing can be said about nothing. For a discussion of the Buddhist conception of the emptiness of Suchness *see:* D.T. Suzuki, *Outlines of Mahayana Buddhism,* pp. 99-124.

10. Buddhists have long held that the world of *samsara*, i.e., the world of constant change which we perceive, is illusion, That is to say, for the unenlightened the world appears as composed of discrete entities within a fixed space-time continuum. Only when man's subjective ignorance (*maya*) is removed does he know the unity of the whole. Cf. Robert Powell, *Zen and Reality* (New York: Viking Press, 1975), pp. 57-60.

11. Edward T. Hall writes:

> It has long been believed that experience is what all men share, that it is always possible somehow to bypass language and culture and to refer back to experience in order to reach another human being. This implicit (and often explicit) belief concerning man's relation to experience was based on the assumption that, when two human beings are subject to the same 'experience,' virtually the same data are being fed to the two central nervous systems and that the two brains record similarly.
>
> Proxomic research casts serious doubt on the validity of this assumption, particularly when the cultures are different. . . . People from different cultures not only speak different languages but, what is possibly more important, inhabit different sensory worlds. Selective screening of sensory data admits some things while filtering out others, so that experience as it is perceived through one set of culturally patterned sensory screens is quite different from experience perceived through another.
>
> Edward T. Hall, *The Hidden Dimension* (Garden City, N. J.: Doubleday and Co., 1969), p. 2.

12. Mircea Eliade, *Shamanism,* trans, Willard Trask (Princeton, N. J.: Princeton University Press, 1965), pp. 33-66 *et passim.*

13. For instance, George Berkeley, the 18th Century British philosopher, carefully analyzed the nature of the so-called "external world" but then quite blythly took the reality of the Self for granted. David Hume, happily, was more circumspect about this point, refusing to grant knowledge of either the external world or the self.

Buddhist philosophy also goes beyond Berkeley. One of the cornerstones of Buddhist thought is the doctrine of *anatta* or "no self." Buddhism quite rigorously maintains that the self or ego is just as illusory as the perceived world. In fact, it is a part of the world of perception. Cf. Edward Conze, *Buddhism: Its Essence and Development* (New York: Harper and Row, 1959), pp. 18-26; D. T. Suzuki, *Outlines of Mahayana Buddhism*, pp. 140-180;
T. R. V. Murti, *The Central Philosophy of Buddhism*, p. 18 ff.

14. Buddhist philosophy says that the self is composed of five *skandas*:
   The Body
   Feelings
   Perceptions
   Impulses and Emotions
   Acts of Consciousness

At death these five are dispersed. There is no continuation of the ego.

15. Sir Isaac Newton, among others, retained an important place in his cosmology for God. Whether God exists or not, scientific experience since his time has demonstrated that science can get on quite admirably without any overt theological presuppositions. Whether they are covertly smuggled in with such notions as natural law is a question which need not concern us unduly here.

16. A coined word from the Latin *ludo, ludere*, "to play, sport, frolic, make love." Cf. J. Huizinga, *Homo Ludens* (Boston: Beacon Press, 1955).

17 The reader should note well, however, that no positive metaphysical statements are intended.

18. A good discussion of early modern scientific (and common sense) views of time and space is to be found in: E. A. Burtt, *The Metaphysical Foundations of Modern Physical Science* (Garden City, N. Y.: Doubleday and Co., 1954), p. 93 ff.

19. D. T. Suzuki, *Outlines of Mahayana Buddhism*, pp. 99-124.

20. Lao Tzu, *Tao Teh Ching*, Chp. 1, 56.

21. *Neti, neti* means literally, "no, no." For instance, Ashvagosha says, "Suchness is neither that which is existence nor that which is non-existence; neither that which is at once existence and non-existence, nor that which is not at once existence and non-existence; it is

neither that which is unity nor that which is at once unity and plurality, nor that which is not at once unity and plurality." From *The Awakening of Faith* as quoted by D. T. Suzuki, *Outlines of Mahayana Buddhism*, p. 102. Cf. T. R. V. Murti, *The Central Philosophy of Buddhism*, p. 154 ff.

22. I am keenly aware that there are still many readers who may think of a myth as simply a silly, false story designed only to delude or entertain. This has been a caricature of myth perpetrated by both modern science and much Christian theology.

Happily, a whole host of thinkers—Jung, Campbell, Levi-Strauss, Neuman, and Eliade, to mention only a few—have done much to destroy this old misunderstanding. Needless to say, in this work the term myth is not used pejoratively. On the contrary, a basic assumption is made that although myths may or may not be factual, they do, if they are true myths, point invariably to truth.

23. This image comes from Alan Watts, *Myth and Ritual in Christianity* (Boston: Beacon Press, 1971), pp. 57-71.

24. Hopefully most philosophers have now gotten over the habit of sneering at all but "factual truth." Nevertheless, in some circles truth is still thought of as something one can demonstrate or verify, the way one verifies that the grass is green.

Such has little to do with truth as it has been traditionally understood, however. Fact has to do with what has already happened. Truth, involves purpose, value, and meaning.

2. LOGOS

1. The concept of the hero is not particularly Buddhist, though it is surely not absent in Buddhist mythology. Much of what is said about the hero in this book was prompted by Joseph Campbell, *Hero with a Thousand Faces* (New York: World Publishing Co., 1970).

There is no need to accept everything Campbell says in order to appreciate many of his central points about hero myths. Surely, Yeshua conforms in many ways to the archetypal pattern which Campbell lays out for us.

2. The Unknown in the Gospels appears to us behind at least three *persona* or masks. John's Gospel comes very close to tearing away the masks and hence trying to see the unseeable.

In Mahayana Buddhism the Unknown can be indicated either

through the historical Buddha (*Nirmanakaya*), the mythic realm of supernatural powers (*Sambhogakaya*), or as the undefinable Unknown (*Dharmakaya*). Cf. T. R. V. Murti, *The Central Philosophy of Buddhism*, p. 284.

3. Despite most translators to the contrary, I believe the first verse should be translated, "In the beginning was the Word, and the Word was to (*pros*) God, and the Word was God." That is to say, this Word is directed from *Theos* to *Theos*.

4. What some call "astral projection" is a peculiar form of self-transcendence in which the self becomes momentarily separated from its body and sees the body from without. Even without such an extreme experience, most of us sense at times a strange sort of detachment from our bodies and even from our egos.

> One day a teacher of meditation (guru) told one of his pupils to walk to the far end of the room and back and sit down. Then he asked:
> "What were you doing just now? Were you walking?"
> The pupil went over his action mentally, and observed everything that he had done and then replied:
> "I was not walking. I was watching the body walk."
> Next the teacher held up a flower and asked him to meditate upon it for a few minutes. After this had been done the teacher questioned:
> "What were you doing just now? Were you meditating?"
> After due observation and reflection the pupil answered:
> "I was not meditating. I was watching the mind meditate."
>
> Ernest Wood, *Yoga*, p. 71.

5. D. T. Suzuki writes,

> The *Dharmakaya*, which literally means "body or system of being," is, according to the Mahayanists the ultimate reality that underlies all particular phenomena; it is that which makes the existence of individuals possible; it is the *raisen d'etre* of the universe; it is the norm of being, which regulates the course of events and thoughts. . . .
>
> All particular existences acquire their meaning only when they are thought of in their oneness in the *Dharmakaya*. The veil of *Maya*, i.e., subjective ignorance, may temporally throw an obstacle to our perceiving the universal light of *Dharmakaya*, in which we are all one. But when our *Bodhi* or intellect, which is by the way a reflection of the *Dharmakaya* in the human mind, is so fully enlightened, we no more build the artificial barrier be-

fore our spiritual eyes; the distinction between *meum* and *teum* is obliterated, no dualism throws the nets of entanglement over us; I recognize myself in you and you recognize yourself in me; *tat tvam asi*. D. T. Suzuki, *Outlines of Mahayana Buddhism*, pp. 45-47.

6. The use of metaphor here is, I trust, obvious.

7. This may be the reason why frequently the most popular religions are those which demand the most by way of concrete action. The religiously submissive person hardly wants a God who demands little or nothing. He wants at least a few stiff demands which he can hardly fulfill at all.

8. Paul Tillich defined religion as an expression of man's Ultimate Concern. Buddhism might, on the other hand, define itself as the extinguishing of concern, especially concern for the self.

9. This claim will certainly be disputed by those who remember that Yeshua is quoted as having said that the first and greatest commandment demands loving God with all one's heart, soul, and mind (Matt. 22:37). It is noteworthy, however, that this is the only place in the Gospels that Yeshua so much as mentions man's love for God. Furthermore, he goes on to qualify this commandment by indicating that the way to fulfill it is to show agape to the neighbor. In other words, Yeshua begins with a commandment well-known to his contemporaries and then reinterprets it to teach a decidedly different message.

10. Cf. D. T. Suzuki, *Outlines of Mahayana Buddhism*. p. 362 ff. and Edward Conze, *Buddhism: Its Essence and Development*, pp. 152-53.

3. WATER AND WIND

1. F. H. Woods, "Deluge," in *Encyclopedia of Religion and Ethics*, ed. James Hastings, 13 Vols. (New York: Charles Scribner's Sons, 1912), IV, pp. 545-557.

2. It is true that none of the usual Hebrew words for sin is employed in the Genesis flood story itself. Rather, the terms used are "wickedness" and "evil imagination" (Gen. 6:5), "corruption" and "violence" (Gen. 6:11). All of these, however, may be grouped under the general category of sin.

3. Because of the emphasis upon the holiness of God's name and the sacredness of his being, Jews continually used (and use) circumlocutions when speaking of him. Hence, "heaven" was employed as a way of referring to God during this period. The kingdom (reign) of God and of heaven are functionally equivalent.

4. For John, the fiery wrath to come is a hidden secret of which men like the Pharisees ought not to be aware.

5. Throughout the Bible this double meaning of both *ruach* (Hebrew) and *pneuma* (Greek) is emphasized. Two further examples (from the many that might be offered) are found in Genesis 1:2 and John 3:5-8. In the former, the wind which moves over the primordial waters is thought of as God's breath. In the latter, Yeshua himself pictures rebirth as like the inhaling of a new wind or breath.

   Parenthetically, it is interesting that in both Hindu and Buddhist forms of yoga *pranayama*, breath control, plays a significant role. Cf. Ernest Wood, *Yoga*, pp. 80-105.

6. John 8:58.

7. This is his title. The text might be better translated, "This is my son, the Beloved One, in whom I rejoice." Yeshua is revealed as *Agapetos*, i.e., that which the Father loves in the world.

8. For a very lucid and rigorous presentation *see*, John Calvin, *The Institutes of the Christian Religion*, Book III, Chapter XXI.

9. The New Testament frequently uses common words in peculiar ways. Rather consistently its authors speak, not of believing in, but of believing into. Many translations unfortunately blur this distinction; yet it remains important nonetheless. The use of *éis* (into) is unusual and therefore must have been purposefully used.

   Faith into implies bridging that gap between subject and object and crossing over into that realm of light. It is significant that John never uses faith as a noun, but speaks continually of it as a verb. Faith is not a thing to possess. Faith is an action, a crossing, a reunification.

10. A good bibliography for and analysis of the Jewish apocalyptic tradition is to be found in: D. S. Russell, *The Method and Message of Jewish Apocalyptic* (Philadelphia, Westminster Press, 1964).

11. Admittedly it is often difficult to tell whether apocalyticists speak of historical events in veiled, symbolical terms or whether they are using quasi-historical symbols to describe ahistorical, spiritual phenomena.

12. By the time of Yeshua there had already developed in Judaism an elaborate oral interpretation of the Torah. Eventually this oral tradition became codified as the Mishna of Judah haNasi and then, with

the addition of the Gemara, as the Talmud. During the first century not all Jews accepted this oral law as binding and there were many disputes as to what should be included in it. Certainly for the Pharisees, however, the Oral Law had become central for their teachings.

13. One of the curious features of many so-called dreams and hallucinations is that they frequently take place upon very similar landscapes. For instance, men the world over have seen in visions a three-storied universe with heaven above and hell below. The more one deals with such phenomena, the more it seems possible that various forms of sense deprivation and/or stimulation simply open the mind to a landscape which, though quite universal, is normally closed to us.

14. Yeshua does not seem to have consistently practiced any of the usual austerities of a holy man. Frequently, we see him eating and drinking without thought for asceticism. (Cf. Matt. 11:19)

15. This may be one of the reasons for the frightening crime rate in the United States. One can overemphasize this theory, of course, for surely there are poorer countries with plenty of crime.

16. Mark 2:1 ff.

17. Matt. 5:40-42.

18. The path of Gautama Siddhartha is also described as the Middle Path. Like Yeshua he forsakes the life of rigorous austerity and counsels moderation in all things.

19. That man has an inner eye (s) which can be opened is a very common idea, particularly in south, central, and east Asia. Yeshua also implies awareness of that eye which can be activated to the divine light. In fact, his cures for blindness frequently seem to serve as parables about that inner eye. Cf. K. Venhata Ramanan, *Nagarjuna's Philosophy as presented in the Maha-Prajna-paramita Sastra* (Rutland, Vt.: Charles E. Tuttle Co., 1966), pp. 119-126.

20. Matt. 22:15-22.

4. THE WAY

1. From an historical point of view these sayings were doubtless not delivered as a sermon. Nevertheless, the author of Matthew put them together to form one consistent discourse. Hence, from the point of view of mythology this is a sermon. What we find in it is not

an expansion upon a few ideas but a crystallization of Yeshua's central teachings. Each saying is meant to be memorized and then explored and elaborated by the hearer. Thus Yeshua's technique is precisely the opposite of most modern preachers. His object is to say much in as few words as possible.

2. The word *ptochoi*, which is usually translated "poor" might be better rendered "beggars." English translators of these Beatitudes consistently seem to soften Yeshua's harsh language.

3. Matt. 19:21.

4. This has been the traditional approach of Roman Catholic theology. Such an interpretation does at least take seriously Yeshua's commands, but it also implies a sort of second-class citizenship for ordinary Christians.

5. Protestants following Luther have generally interpreted Yeshua as saying these things in order to prompt a reaction of repentance for sin. Rather than seeking perfection, which is beyond the grasp of sinful men, Protestant Christians recognize the inevitability of sin and forgiveness. This approach, however, hardly seems to do justice to Yeshua's words, for he spends little time promising forgiveness for those who repent. His emphasis throughout is upon the possibility of new life.

6. He doesn't say that men may become the light; he says, you *are* the light.

7. Another example of Yeshua's penchant to equate the reconciliation of men with the reconciliation of man and God.

8. Recently there has been a spate of books and articles related to the possibility that Yeshua himself was married. It may well be that the historical Yeshua was married but it is also clear that the mythical Yeshua of the Gospels was not. It is the latter who has been important for Christianity, not the former.

9. When Adam was created he was both male and female together in one body. Because he was lonesome, God divided him in two. Marriage is a reconstitution of that Adam. (Gen. 2:18-25)

10. It is interesting to see how modern exegetes who want to find in the New Testament a very positive attitude toward sex rationalize about this passage. Very few are willing to take Yeshua's words at face value.

11. In Japanese, *satori*. D. T. Suzuki, *Zen Buddhism: Selected Writings of D. T. Suzuki*. ed. William Barrett (Garden City, N. Y.: Doubleday and Co., 1956), pp. 83-108. See also: Heinrich Dumolin, *A History of Zen Buddhism*, trans. Paul Prachey (Boston: Beacon Press, 1969), p. 249.

12. I use the term "religion" in a non-technical and rather loosely de-

fined way to suggest those institutions and practices whereby man relates himself to whatever he believes divine.

13. The word in Greek is plural, as it would have been in both Aramaic and Hebrew. There seems to be no good reason to render it in the singular.

14. Despite its radical skepticism about the gods and the supernatural in general, Buddhism also speaks mythically about various heavens and hells. In fact, there are many striking similarities between Buddhist and Christian images of the two regions. Buddhists, however, are usually clearer about their use of symbolic language. They indulge in all sorts of myths and metaphors but also insist that these are creations of man's imagination. Cf., for instance, Daigan and Alicia Matsunaga, *The Buddhist Concept of Hell* (New York: Philosophical Library, 1972).

15. Yeshua repeatedly used monetary images in his teaching. Cf., for instance, Matt. 13:44-46, 20:1-15; Luke 12:13-21, 14:29-33, 15:8-10, 16:1-13, etc.

16. For a good collection of writings about Buddhist meditation practices, *see* Edward Conze, *Buddhist Scriptures*, pp. 98-144. For a more technical description *see* Edward Conze, *Buddhist Meditation* (New York: Harper and Row, 1956).

17. Obviously, Yeshua is not speaking simply about our physical eyes but of another kind of illumination of which our physical eyes are but metaphors.

18. This is very similar to the sort of life the Buddhist monk attempts to live.

19. For a good discussion of the Buddhist view of *karma, see* D. T. Suzuki, *Outlines of Mahayana Buddhism*, pp. 181-216.

20. Kismet is the Islamic word for fate.

21. Edward Conze writes, "It is indeed a cherished belief among Buddhists that meditation not only widens the range of our spiritual awareness, but also adds one dimension or more to our actual existence, by awakening our psychic and supernatural gifts. These occult powers of the more advanced saints are a stock item of all Buddhist writing." Edward Conze, *Buddhist Scriptures*, pp. 98-99. *See also* John Blofeld, *The Tantric Mysticism of Tibet* (New York: E. P. Dutton and Co., 1970), pp. 221-225. And, for a wild-eyed view of the mysteries of Tibet, *see* Alexandra David-Neel, *Magic and Mystery in Tibet* (Baltimore: Penguin Books, 1971), passim.

22. This is not to say that this power is "unnatural" to man. Rather it is man's civilization and life style—his ego—which rob him of powers which are rightfully his. True faith simply allows those powers to be recovered.

23. Hence they are placed in a footnote in most modern translations.

5. THE DISCIPLES AND THE CHRIST

1. Christian Gnostics generally claimed to perpetuate the esoteric teachings of Yeshua and, because of their claims, were strongly countered by more orthodox churchmen. Simply because some Gnostic teachings seem to bear little relation to the Christianity we know, however, we ought not to assume either that the Gnostics were always wrong or that Yeshua taught nothing secretly. The fact that one party in the church triumphed over another does not imply anything about the truth of either position.
2. Matt. 10:19-20.
3. It is interesting, parenthetically, that this word comes from the same root as mathematics. In effect, mathematics in the Western world has become equated with a study of number and number theories because Plato believed that contemplation of numbers and geometrical forms is the best way to find illumination. The mathematics of Yeshua are found in the Sermon on the Mount.
4. According to ancient notions, each moon of the year, in fact each day, is a distinct being.
5. In Luke 10:1-12 Yeshua later sends out 70 (in some versions 72) disciples on a similar mission. That is to say, he sends out 12x6 disciples.
6. Matt. 10:25.
7. To be sure, offering Peace (Shalom) was an ordinary practice in those days, but the text implies that the Peace of the disciples was more than the usual, verbal sort.
8. Luke 9:60-62. Very few modern Christian theologians have come to grips with these teachings at all.
9. Yeshua usually speaks of Gehenna, not Hades. Gehenna was a garbage dump outside of Jerusalem and symbolizes well the worthlessness of ego-life.
10. Attributed to Lichtenberg by Kierkegaard. Soren Kierkegaard, *Stages on Life's Way*, trans. Walter Lowrie (New York: Schocken Books, 1969), p. 26.
11. Much ink has been spilled about Yeshua's "Messianic Secret." Clearly he did not go around proclaiming himself Messiah.

12. Caesarea Philippi was a pagan city located on the lower slopes of Mt. Hermon. It was known for an important cave shrine which the Greeks had dedicated to Pan and the nymphs.

13. In the Gospel of John, Andrew, the brother of Peter, identifies Yeshua as Messiah very early in the story. (John 1:41)

14. I Samuel 16:12-13.

15. II Samuel 7:14, Psalm 89:26-27.

16. For further discussion of apocalyptic elements in the gospels, *see* Chapter VI.

17. Eliade observes, "The mountain, because it is the meeting place of heaven and earth, is situated at the centre of the world, and is of course the highest point of the earth. That is why so many sacred places—'holy places,' temples, palaces, holy towns—are likened to 'mountains' and are themselves made 'centres,' become in some magic way part of the summit of the cosmic hill." Mircea Eliade, *Patterns of Comparative Religion*, trans. Rosemary Sheed (New York: World Publishing Co., 1966), p. 100.

   Mount Sumeru and Vulture Peak both serve as holy mountains in the Buddhist tradition. Many of the Sutras are delivered by the Buddha on a holy mountain.

18. The word for transfiguration in the Greek Testament is metamorpho'o.

19. Peter is identified as first among equals in Matthew 10:2. If this list represents a hierarchical ordering of disciples, then Peter and Judas stand at opposite ends of the scale. Throughout the gospels, Peter seems to speak for the twelve.

20. I Cor. 10:1-4.

21. John 14:6.

22. It is significant how quickly the ego can take such a claim to universality and turn it into an ego-prop for a particular tradition.

23. Mircea Eliade, *Patterns of Comparative Religion*, pp. 265-278.

24. Yehezkel Kaufmann, *The Religion of Israel from its beginnings to the Babylonian exile*, trans. and abridged by Moshe Greenberg (New York, Schocken Books, 1972), pp. 7-20.

   Because Israelite attacks upon paganism were limited in scope, if not in vehemence, Kaufmann concludes that Israel actually knew very little about the religions of her neighbors. Although such a conclusion is possible, it seems more reasonable to conclude that Israelites regarded only certain features of paganism deplorable.

6. THE LAST THINGS

1. The Apostles' Creed, for instance, merely outlines the chief events of his life: born, suffered, died, buried, descended, resurrected, ascended. No mention is made of his teachings.
2. The word passion derives probably from Pascha or Pescha, the Hebrew name for Passover. It has nothing to do with passionate emotions as we now think of them.
3. Zech. 9:9.
4. Palms do not grow in hilly Jerusalem. Therefore palm branches would have to have been imported from the lowlands, as they were for the festival of Tabernacles (Succoth) when palms and citrons were used together ceremonially.
5. After years of discontent the Jews finally erupted in rebellion in the late 60's A. D. At first their efforts were successful but eventually the Roman legions had their way. Jerusalem was sacked and destroyed, the Temple was completely demolished and Jewish nationalistic hopes were dashed. Another rebellion occurred in the early second century under Bar Kochba with equally devastating results for the Jews.
6. As usual the Gospels pick up a theme from the Jewish tradition—this time, the resurrection of the dead—and then completely transform it. What is raised is not the old ego but Christ. In the Buddhist tradition it is only those who are unenlightened who are trapped by the inexorable law of karma. Those who have crossed over know that they are free. By the same token, only those who cling to the ego face the last judgment and need to fear hell. Relinquish the ego and the resurrection is accomplished already.
7. Gen. 9:4.
8. This interpretation sees the words of institution as very much like a Zen ko'an. Trevor Ling defines the ko'an as, "A technical term used in Zen Buddhism for an exercise given by a Zen master to his disciple and designed to break through intellectual limitations and lead to a flash of sudden intuition for attainment of satori. The ko'an are often couched as problems insolvable by, and nonsensical to, the intellect. In almost all of them the striking element is the illogical or absurd act or word." Trevor Ling, A Dictionary of Buddhism (New York: Charles Scribner's Sons, 1972) pp. 159-60. Parenthetically, it might be added that many of the sayings of Jesus, particularly in the Gospel of John seem to function as ko'an. One thinks, for instance, of his conversation with Nicodemus in John 3:1-21. For a more extended

treatment of the *ko'an* see: D. T. Suzuki, *Zen Buddhism: Selected Writings of D. T. Suzuki*, pp. 132-154.

9. Matt. 26:38.
10. Lao Tzu, *Tao Teh Ching*, Ch. 47.
11. Gen. 3:1-7. The curse of man is to have the knowledge of good and evil and hence, inevitably to judge both the world and himself.

7. RESURRECTION BEYOND THE END

1. One should not read into "I am" any egoistical or even personal qualities. Perhaps simply "am" would be better.
2. Zen Buddhists like Suzuki sometimes speak of the experience of *satori* but normally conclude by saying that it is really not an experience after all. D. T. Suzuki, *Zen Buddhism: Selected Writings of D. T. Suzuki*, pp. 83-108, 219.
3. D. T. Suzuki, *Outlines of Mahayana Buddhism*, pp. 331-371.

INDEX